Publications of the

National Bureau of Economic Research, Inc.

Number 44

National Product in Wartime

National Product
in
Wartime

Simon Kuznets

NATIONAL BUREAU OF ECONOMIC RESEARCH, INC.

New York 1945

Contents

Preface

WHEN carefully examined, estimates of national product[1] are seen to be compounds of statistical data of varying accuracy based upon assumptions concerning the purpose, value, and scope of economic activity. These assumptions must be kept clearly in mind since they affect the estimates and their meaning much more than do inaccuracies in the statistical data.

National product may be defined as the total net contribution of economic activity in a nation. But this definition cannot have a precise meaning, or the total a unique value, unless the underlying assumptions are specified. *Contribution* has meaning only in terms of definite ends. *Net* assumes a distinction between goods that satisfy the ends directly and those that serve them indirectly, through entering other, final, goods. Confining the concept to *economic* activity implies a distinction between it and activities that may satisfy the same ends but cannot be classified as economic. A *total* net contribution assumes some scheme by which qualitatively different final products are given comparable and additive weights. Finally, reference to the *nation* implies its separate entity, to whose ends, as postulated, economic activities are directed, rather than to those of mankind at large.

Specifying these underlying assumptions raises many thorny problems even in peacetime. As they have been discussed at length in the national income literature,[2] to deal with them here would be superfluous. We note merely that the problems arise largely from the conflict between the aim of the investigator and the recalcitrant nature of reality. The investigator desires and society needs estimates of national product comparable within a nation from period to period, between nations, and composed of comparable parts at

[1] The term is used here synonymously with national income in order to emphasize the real contents rather than the dollar aggregates in changing prices.

[2] See, among others, the author's *National Income and Its Composition* (National Bureau of Economic Research, 1941), I, Ch. 1, and the six volumes of *Studies in Income and Wealth* (National Bureau of Economic Research), particularly I, II, III, and VI.

any given time. Yet such estimates can be made only under assumptions that reduce to a common denominator the various sectors of an economy at any given time, or of the nation's economy at different times, or of the economies of different nations. The differences in these elements shift over time and across space. This complexity of observable reality compels the investigator to select one set of assumptions from among many concerning the purpose, value, and scope of economic activity. No matter what assumptions are adopted, so long as they are stable in space and time violence is done to the complexity and heterogeneity of the aspects of social activity that are essentially economic. Consequently, there is always room for disagreement whether a given set of assumptions is less or more applicable in view of the uses to which the estimates are to be put.

Obviously, a major war magnifies these conceptual difficulties, raising questions concerning the ends economic activity is made to pursue. It influences, partly through the effect on the ends and partly in other ways, the distinction between intermediate and final products and thereby between net and gross national product. It shifts markedly the boundaries of free market institutions, of government controlled activities, of the family and of other institutions. And it accentuates the degree to which national interest is permitted to determine the scope of national product.

We consider some of the conceptual problems in estimating national product raised or magnified by war, and attempt to apply the tentative solutions worked out in measuring changes in it during World Wars I and II. In Part I we discuss the interpretation of war output as a component of national product viewed as a sum of final goods, i.e., goods satisfying directly the purposes of economic activity. Does war production satisfy wants of ultimate consumers, in this case merged in an entity called the 'nation', and is it therefore on a par with the flow of consumer goods? Or should war output be classified under capital formation—investment needed to sustain or augment the capacity of the nation's economy to produce goods in the future? Should the aims served directly by war production—defense of the nation's social institutions or attainment of what is deemed its proper place in the world—be classified as themselves ends, on a par with the provision of consumer goods? Or should they be put first? Each position is illustrated statistically, and the one singled out that seems most appropriate either for the shorter term of a major war or for the longer term that would span both peace and war.

In Part II the ways in which war and nonwar production is priced are contrasted. War and peace type products (or resources entering them) cannot be added into a national product total until the differences in their valuation due to differences in the institutional mechanisms that determine their respective market prices are corrected for. Though the problem is clear, its solution is far from easy. The statistical analysis, for the five years associated with this war, yields several variants, selection among which is necessarily a matter of judgment. But they suggest a basis for translating the economic experience of wartime, affected as it is by the circumstances of a concentrated effort to win a war, into terms comparable with peacetime, so that what has happened can be appraised and interpreted as part of the longer term changes that may persist in the foreseeable future.

In Part III changes in national product and in its chief components during World Wars I and II are compared. For each, five years are covered—1914-18 and 1939-43. Despite the differences in the character of the two wars, several striking parallels can be observed: in the growth of national product, in the increase in the share of war output, in the greater importance of manufacturing, in the distribution of income by type and by size. On the other hand, during this war the increase in national product and in the share of war output was bigger, the emphasis on manufacturing more conspicuous, and the shift in the distribution of income payments in favor of service incomes more striking. All these similarities and differences should help us to understand the nature of the readjustments that will have to be faced after this war.

One wishes that the conceptual problems could be resolved without recourse to alternatives and variants; and that statistical analysis would admit of unequivocal conclusions, which could then provide a firm factual basis for understanding what has happened and perhaps for considerations of policy. To the degree that the problems are not resolved and the statistical analysis yields several variants rather than a single estimate, this report is merely a halfway house from which we cannot as yet remove the scaffolding of alternative assumptions and estimates.

This is due only in part to inadequacy of data, which forces one to make various guesses instead of a single reliable estimate. It is due even more to a conscious allowance for the possible validity of different viewpoints and divergent assumptions. Confining oneself to a single viewpoint and to a corresponding single series of estimates would be convenient. However, as national product is a concept that implies answers to problems over which social philosophers have wrangled from time immemorial, the price might be too high.

In preparing this monograph, I have been aided by colleagues at the War Production Board and the National Bureau of Economic Research. To whatever work was done, on the subjects discussed here, while I was associated with the War Production Board, Frederick M. Cone, Loring Wood, and Jacob Grauman contributed much. In piecing out the estimates and making the analysis I have profited, as always, from the expert assistance of Lillian Epstein and Elizabeth Jenks. The ready cooperation of the Department of Commerce, in putting its estimates at our disposal and helping to interpret them, facilitated our task materially.

Suggestions by other colleagues and friends, particularly Thor Hultgren and Geoffrey Moore of the National Bureau staff, were of great benefit. Harold M. Groves and Oswald Knauth of the National Bureau's Board of Directors; Gerhard Colm of the Bureau of the Budget; Morris A. Copeland of the War Production Board; Everett E. Hagen of the Federal Reserve Board; and W. S. Woytinsky of the Social Security Board raised questions that led to other improvements. Martha Anderson has edited the manuscript with her customary patience and attention, bettering its style and making it more readable. To all these my hearty thanks.

Whatever elements of judgment are involved in the conclusions submitted below—and I have tried to identify these elements— are to be attributed to me as an individual observer and student, not as representing in any way either the War Production Board or the National Bureau of Economic Research; nor should these judgments be attributed to any of the colleagues and friends who commented on the manuscript.

SIMON KUZNETS

March 1945

PART I
Treatment of War Output

1 VIEWPOINTS ON WAR OUTPUT

A major war alters the emphasis on the ends to which the productive system of a country is geared in peacetime. Different interpretations of this shift in emphasis lead to different treatments of war output, and estimates of national product will vary accordingly. We can assume that the huge drafts war production makes upon the country's resources represent a new purpose of economic activity, on a par with the one dominant in peacetime—supplying goods to ultimate consumers; or that this new purpose—providing commodities and services for the armed conflict—should be considered paramount during a major war; or that the peacetime aim of economic activity should be retained in war and supplying the armed conflict be treated as subordinate to it.

Before weighing these viewpoints and illustrating their effects statistically we consider other possible positions which seem at first to remove the necessity of choosing among several goals of economic activity. If national product could be estimated without making essentially arbitrary decisions concerning purposes, it would obviously be extremely desirable.[1]

[1] When in subsequent discussion we speak interchangeably of ultimate 'purposes', 'ends', 'goals', and 'objectives' we refer to the productive outcome of a nation's economy so far as it is intended and approved by the operative controls. Such aims are revealed by the functional scheme of the total economic system, whether set up by direct governmental action or established by long standing custom. It is not easy to formulate such aims consistently for periods during which an economy's functions and problems have been radically altered or for societies with widely divergent patterns of organization and diverse problems attacked by economic means. Yet by undertaking to estimate national product, i.e., the contribution of the economy to the achievement of the intended and approved aims, the statistician implies that he has a clear idea of what the society wants. While he may ease the burden of choice by making several formulations and calculating corresponding variants of national product, each variant implies some set of ultimate objectives. Reluctant as he may be to pose as a social philosopher and pass judgment upon the net result of the economic activities of millions of individuals, that is in fact what a national income estimator does, even when he tries to base his judgment upon a recognizable consensus of the society whose economy he is studying.

Obviously the terms 'purposes', 'ends', 'goals' as used here do not mean a sum total of the immediate aims of the individuals who participate actively in the economy. Probably most individuals are driven by the necessity to earn a living; some may seek economic gain as a basis for social prestige, others may be impelled by the instinct of workmanship or by a desire to render service to society; some may take a job from sheer boredom; and perhaps the great majority are animated by a mixture of motives. Even were it possible to add the immediate motives of individuals and strike a weighted average, the result would not be equivalent to the objectives to which the nation's economy is actually directed. Many societies, notably those organized democratically, leave a wide area for self-seeking individual initiative in the expectation of

a) It might be argued that war production, like the flow of goods to individuals and households, is determined largely by consumers, and that its growth to astronomical heights in a major war is due to a shift in public taste. True, taste is expressed in this case through the government rather than through market demands by individual purchasers. But even in peacetime consumers register some of their wants through the government; for example, for more schools or parks. The flow of goods to the armed conflict could then be interpreted as directly satisfying desires of ultimate consumers; i.e., as a new category in the flow of consumer goods. And just as we include in national product the full value of goods flowing to individuals and households, we would include the full value of goods flowing to the armed conflict.

This position is unassailable in formal logic, *if* we are free to interpret the wishes of ultimate consumers as we please. But we are not to the point of indulging in arbitrary imputations. Even in peacetime, consumers may be provided with goods through decisions by the government; but chiefly in the form of services directly related to the needs or wants of individuals and households (e.g., education, recreation). A decision to engage in a major war can hardly be motivated by a desire to instruct or amuse members of the armed forces and employees of war agencies; or to supply thrills to ultimate consumers by parading guns, airplanes, or battleships, or writing accounts of battles as sports events. And if it has other motivations, e.g., to preserve a social order cherished by a nation, and is thus a species of capital investment, then surely it cannot be interpreted in terms of tastes of ultimate consumers. If it could, so could all intermediate production in peacetime as well as all capital formation. Any product could then be considered final; for example, all ingot steel could be classified as a final product because steelmakers presumably make it at the behest of ultimate consumers.

b) To the extreme of saying that a collective decision to engage in a major war is on a par with the ordinary expressions of consumers' tastes in peacetime markets, the other extreme can be

Note 1 concluded:
public good. Society may tolerate the means for the sake of the gains. Adam Smith's theory of the unseen hand, that private selfishness works public benefit, still rules, if with many limitations, the democratic economy.

opposed: to view war production from the vantage of an assumed ideal organization of the world economy. If, for example, all international disputes were settled by peaceful means, and if no nation were concerned to amass instruments of war in order to challenge this mode of settlement, war production, should that be still conceivable, would add nothing whatever to national product, except so far as it might become available for nonwar consumption.

The advantage of appraising economic activity by criteria independent of the changing and mixed purposes pursued in the real world cannot be gainsaid. It might give new insight, a new basis for appraisal, and goals for reorienting society's approach to the economic and social problems of the day. But the estimate would not be one of national product as commonly thought of—the net contribution of economic activity to the goals of the United States in the 20th century. Society, as organized today, no more precludes armed conflict among nations than it forbids advertising food products of little or no value according to scientifically established standards of nutrition, or prevents the growth of huge urban centers on which scarce resources must be lavished to relieve the incommodities of congestion. So long as we attempt to measure the contribution of economic activity to what within the *national* framework are actually accepted as ends, war output cannot be dismissed as completely irrelevant and omitted without further ado from national product.

c) We might treat war as an unforecastable natural calamity, for which no calculable current provision can be made. Losses sustained in such disasters in peacetime are usually debited to the capital account, and are excluded from depreciation, depletion, and other costs that can be currently planned for and calculated; i.e., they are excluded from current capital consumption in the income account. Consequently, goods produced to replace losses occasioned by such natural calamities are fully included in net national product.[2] By analogy, losses due to war, in the way of destruction of assets, would be entered in the capital account; but the income account, i.e., net national product, would include war output as fully as it includes capital formation intended to replace losses

[2] See Solomon Fabricant, *Capital Consumption and Adjustment* (National Bureau of Economic Research, 1938), pp. 9-11, especially his references to Pigou's writings on the subject, p. 10, notes 4 and 5.

from natural calamities in peacetime—at gross value with the rather minor deduction of depreciation on war construction (i.e., plants producing munitions and military housing).

This viewpoint is akin to that discussed under (b), in the sense that it rejects an integral connection between the incidence of war and the organization of the nation's economic and social system, just as the viewpoint under (b) denies war as a pattern of behavior in an ideal system of world organization. But, paradoxically, the statistical effect of the position at issue is not to omit war output from national product completely, as is done under (b); but to include it fully, except for the minor item of depreciation on war construction. This different statistical effect is due to the additional assumption that net changes on capital account can be differentiated from capital consumption in the income account.

This position is not discussed for two reasons. First, we cannot bring ourselves to interpret war as a natural calamity rather than as, in large degree, a consequence of our social institutions and, therefore, closely connected with their functioning and costing them heavily. Second, the distinction between the capital and income account is tenable only so long as unforecastable disasters entail a capital loss small in comparison with capital consumption as a production cost in the income account. As losses from natural calamities in peacetime are small, their exclusion from the income account leads to but a minor exaggeration of the total net material product of society. Losses occasioned by major wars are hardly so small; and their complete exclusion from the income account would lead to its inflation to a point that might render it well nigh meaningless as a basis for estimating society's *net* product.

d) Regardless what war production means in terms of purpose, it represents an input of scarce resources of the type utilized in peacetime to turn out economic goods. Indeed, many of these resource units are identical: in the year preceding war they go into finished consumer goods or contribute to the accumulation of peace type capital equipment; and in the years of war are diverted to the production of munitions, war construction, or service in the armed conflict proper. Why then, without worrying about what ends war production is meant to serve, not measure it as a component of national product—as input of resources whose capacity to contribute to *any* accepted purpose is beyond question?

The difficulty is that this position itself already attributes meaning to war output in terms of a peacetime set of purposes. The national product it yields is total resource input, not final output. Resources, however, have meaning only in terms of the set (no matter how diverse) of products the resources are assumed eventually to enter (or produce). To treat war output as the embodiment of resources known to be productive because they are identical with or similar to resources used before the war to turn out final products is to assume that they retain their peacetime meaning, and implicitly to consider war output as a final product equivalent to the products the resources in question enter in peacetime. If such an assumption is made, it had better be explicit and contrasted to the three assumptions suggested at the beginning of this section.

2 WAR OUTPUT AS CAPITAL FORMATION

Estimates of peacetime national product assume that economic activity is to produce goods to satisfy ultimate consumers; that production is for man, not man for production. Accordingly, the distinction between net and gross is clear. Indeed, the fact that provision of consumer goods is viewed as the purpose of economic activity is revealed in the difference between the treatment of the flow of consumer and of capital goods. Because to satisfy consumers is the primary purpose, net national product includes the *gross* value of consumer goods flowing to individuals and households; and because capital goods are subsidiary to this purpose, net national product includes only *net* additions to their stock since net increments alone can augment the future supply of consumer goods.

Given consumer satisfaction as the primary purpose, war production may be treated as an item similar to capital formation in that it serves either to maintain or increase the flow of consumer goods in the future. When intended for defense, war production may be viewed as similar to other capital investment designed to avoid or mitigate the effects of calamities that threaten the productive fabric of the country (flood control, etc.). In a successful aggressor nation, war production, even if designed directly to augment its power, might conceivably lead to an increase in the prospective flow of consumer goods, and may also be treated as a species of capital investment.

If consumer satisfaction is the primary purpose, net national product should include, as in the case of capital formation of a peace type, only such unexpended part of total war output as is a net addition to the inventory of war goods. In statistical practice this means subtracting from the gross value of war output in any given year the current consumption and obsolescence of war goods. In developing illustrative figures, two estimates of such current consumption of war goods were made.

The first assumes that the period between one major war and the next constitutes a major war cycle, and treats the cumulated total of gross war output during this cycle as having been completely consumed. If the purpose of war production is to preserve the independence of a nation, it is fully attained and the goods fully consumed in a period that begins with a threat represented by one major war and ends when another major war offers a new threat. Similarly, if we are estimating the national product of an aggressor nation in a single period of war and peace, whatever investment in war goods has been made is fully consumed, in that a new war entails a new installment of huge investments in war production.

For illustrative purposes, the cycle of World War II is dated from 1939, although it might well have been dated a few years earlier, and we assume that it will last 30 years, i.e., through 1968. We begin with a partly actual, partly hypothetical series of gross war output for this country, and convert it to constant prices. The cumulated total of war output, by definition, is the total consumption of war goods for the World War II cycle. Apportioning this total consumption equally by years, for simplicity's sake, yields an estimate of annual consumption; the difference between gross war output for each year and the average annual consumption is the net addition to the inventory of war goods (Table I 1), the item that enters net national product when war output is treated as a species of capital formation.

Under these assumptions negative capital formation on the war-goods account characterizes all years following the assumed cessation of hostilities and the prewar years in which expanding war output did not reach the average levels for the war cycle as a whole. The stock of war goods is added to only in the few years when war production reaches the pitch of an all-out effort.

If, from a longer range viewpoint, the inevitability or likelihood of major wars is admitted, one must bear in mind not only the large additions to the capital stock of national security made in years of intensive war production, but also the large drafts upon this capital in peace years when war output becomes small. National product, augmented by net additions to war inventory in years of war, is reduced by drafts on the stock of war capital in

TABLE I 1

Gross and Net War Output, World War II Cycle
Annual Consumption assumed Constant throughout
(dollar figures in billions)

| | GROSS WAR OUTPUT | | | NET WAR OUTPUT | |
| | Current prices | Resource input at 1939 prices | IMPLICIT PRICE INDEX | Resource input at 1939 prices | Current prices |
	(1)	(2)	(3)	(4)	(5)
1939	1.4	1.4	100	—10.2	—10.2
1940	2.8	2.5	112	—9.1	—10.2
1941	12.8	9.9	129	—1.7	—2.2
1942	50.3	34.3	147	22.7	33.4
1943	81.3	50.2	162	38.6	62.5
1944	92	56.8	162	45.2	73.2
1945	70	43	162	31.4	50.9
1946	30	19	162	7.4	12.0
1947	...	6	...	—5.6	...
		"		"	
		"		"	
		"		"	
		"		"	
1968	...	6	...	—5.6	...
Total		349.1		0	

COLUMN

1 Actual through 1943 from *Survey of Current Business,* April 1944, p. 13, Table 10, line 4; assumed thereafter through 1946.

2 Col. 1 adjusted by a price index of resource compensation in war output (App. Table II 12) for 1939-43; 100(col. 1 ÷ col. 3) for 1944-46; assumed thereafter.

3 Actual through 1943 (Table II 3); assumed thereafter through 1946.

4 Col. 2 minus average annual consumption during the cycle: the sum of entries in col. 2 divided by the number of years in the cycle (i.e., the 30 years 1939-68).

5 (Col. 4 x col. 3) ÷ 100.

years of peace. The sole way to minimize such a drain on net national product in peacetime is to prolong the period of peace, i.e., to assume a war cycle of such length that the current *annual* consumption of war goods becomes small.

These calculations could be refined by shifting the chronological boundaries of the World War II cycle or by allowing a gradual, rather than sudden, increase in war output between the two cycles. But the conclusions would still be fundamentally the same. For the cycle as a whole, war production could not augment net national product, for the large additions in the years of a major war would be offset by substantial deductions in other years. In the short run, however, it would be positive in the years of a major war, thereby increasing national product, and negative in other years, thereby reducing it.

The second estimate of the current consumption of war goods is based on assigning different life periods to the various categories of war goods.[3] The apportionment of the gross war output postulated for the World War II cycle in Table I 2 is based on rough hypothetical ratios between perishable war goods (services of the armed forces and war agencies, expendable munitions, clothing, etc.) and durable (war plants, war installations such as barracks and air fields, and durable munitions—battleships, aircraft, guns, etc.). We assume that perishable war goods are consumed in the year in which they are produced. To durable goods produced during the war years, that is, 1939-46, we assign a ten-year life; to durable goods produced after 1946, a twenty-year life; for both, straight line depreciation is assumed.

With current consumption thus estimated as the sum of perishable war goods and a corresponding part of the accumulated total of durable war instruments, net additions to the inventory of war goods can be calculated. As in Table I 1, both the addition to the stock of war capital during the war and the deficit in the years immediately following its assumed end are large. Again for the entire war cycle, war production contributes no substantial amount

[3] This basis is much less appropriate for allocating the consumption of the total investment by a nation in peace or in aggressive ambition. But it is similar to the practice followed in private business where separate categories of capital goods, all forming a related complex, are nevertheless subject to depreciation rates based upon different life periods.

TABLE I 2

Gross and Net War Output, World War II Cycle
Consumption based on Three Life Periods
(dollar figures in billions)

	GROSS WAR OUTPUT Resource input at 1939 prices (1)	CONSUMPTION 1939 prices (2)	NET WAR OUTPUT Resource input at 1939 prices (3)	PRICE INDEX (4)	NET WAR OUTPUT Current prices (5)
1939	1.4	0.5	0.9	100	0.9
1940	2.5	1.1	1.4	112	1.6
1941	9.9	4.0	5.9	129	7.6
1942	34.3	13.7	20.6	147	30.3
1943	50.2	22.0	28.2	162	45.7
1944	56.8	27.8	29.0	162	47.0
1945	43	30.6	12.4	162	20.1
1946	19	23.9	—4.9	162	—7.9
1947	6	18.1	—12.1		
1948	6	18.2	—12.2		
1949	6	18.3	—12.3		
1950	6	18.2	—12.2		
1951	6	17.6	—11.6		
1952	6	15.3	—9.3		
1953	6	11.9	—5.9		
1954	6	8.1	—2.1		
1955	6	5.7	0.3		
1956-65 av.	6	5.3	0.7		
1966-68 av.	6	6.0	0		
Total	349.1		23.1		

COLUMN

1 Table I 1, col. 2.

2 Gross war output divided between perishable and durable by assuming the following percentages for perishable: 30 for 1939-44; 40 for 1945; 50 for 1946; and 60 for all later years. It is assumed that perishable goods are consumed in the year in which they are produced. For durable items a 10-year life is assumed for those produced in 1939-46 and a 20-year life for those produced in later years. Within the life periods straight line depreciation is assumed.

3 Col. 1 — col. 2.

4 Table I 1, col. 3.

5 (Col. 3 x col. 4) ÷ 100.

to net national product—in this case because of the short life attributed even to durable war instruments.[4]

[4] The two calculations of the consumption of war goods (Tables I 1 and 2) are illustrative, though the various assumptions as to life, postwar levels of war output,

Given estimates of net war output, we can, for the years since 1939, calculate a net national product in which war output enters as a species of capital formation, i.e., for the maintenance or increase of the flow of consumer goods, and therefore indirectly related to the long run primary purpose of economic activity (Table I 3). The estimates are confined to the years for which actual values of other components of national product were available at the time of writing.

TABLE I 3

Net National Product
War Output treated as Capital Formation
1939-1943
(billions of dollars, current prices)

	1939	1940	1941	1942	1943
1 Flow of goods to consumers	64.8	68.8	77.7	85.1	94.1
2 Nonwar capital formation, net	6.0	9.3	13.0	0.1	—6.5
3 Additions to war capital inventory					
a) Based on Table I 1	—10.2	—10.2	—2.2	33.4	62.5
b) Based on Table I 2	0.9	1.6	7.6	30.3	45.7
4 Net national product (1 + 2 + 3)					
a) Using 3a	60.6	67.9	88.5	118.6	150.1
b) Using 3b	71.7	79.7	98.3	115.5	133.3

Lines 1 & 2 from Table II 1.

Note 4 concluded:

etc., have been assigned values that seem to us realistic. A case could easily be made for other levels, and hence for different estimates. With respect to the notion of war cycles, one might argue that the contribution of one war to the security and progress of a nation is not necessarily fully exhausted by the time the next war occurs, but persists into and beyond it. If we admit this argument, the life period would have to be longer than the one assumed, and total consumption after the second war would be based on the outlays of both wars.

Likewise, in the second calculation, the life assigned to the durable parts of war output could be made much longer than the one assumed; there would then be a substantial residue of net war capital formation on war 1 account even by the time war 2 begins.

Such variations in assumptions introduce no new elements into the analysis; and it did not seem worth while to elaborate the illustrations. It may be admitted that wars do not occur with sufficient regularity and their effects are not so readily measurable as to make it easy to determine the constants needed in calculating the consumption of war goods.

Net national product consists of (a) flow of goods to consumers, (b) net nonwar capital formation, (c) net war output, i.e., net additions to the inventory of war goods. Item (c) is negligible in years like 1939 and 1940, and becomes large and positive in 1942 and 1943. Consequently, the rise in net national product is accelerated, especially between 1941 and 1943.

3 WAR OUTPUT AS FINAL PRODUCT

That war output is, like nonwar capital formation, for the maintenance or increase of the flow of consumer goods is tenable in the long run, but may be challenged in the short span of a major war. When the nation is in danger, military demands are paramount and can hardly be treated as capital formation for the sake of consumers, with the usual implication this conveys of discretion as to which capital investment to make or whether to make it at all. In these periods, short as they may be, the military conflict itself dominates economic activity and war output is properly treated as a final product.

To assume that the *sole* purpose of economic activity is to provide military goods is never valid, not even for the most rigorously controlled war economy. Its logic would demand that consumer goods not needed to maintain, either directly or indirectly, resources embodied in war goods should be viewed as unproductive and hence eliminated; and, likewise, tools for the production of such superfluous commodities and services. With the exception of short periods of a 'besieged fortress' condition, even when absorption in a war effort is intense, an economy never excludes or could exclude completely the demands of everyday life, i.e., of the primary purposes that guide it in the longer run.

Nevertheless we should attempt to see what national product would amount to were the provision of military goods accepted as the sole purpose. Discarding the dominant assumption underlying the customary estimates of peacetime has a marked effect on the totals. Table I 4 illustrates what happens when any goal other than to provide consumer goods is assumed dominant.

The first and chief effect is on measuring the flow of consumer goods, which become merely tools, i.e., means of keeping ultimate consumers alive as potential producers of war goods, of swelling

TABLE I 4

Value of Increases in the Gainfully Occupied and in their Efficiency
1939-1943

	1939	1940	1941	1942	1943
A LONG TERM BASIS					
1 Increase in gainfully occupied, millions	0.7	0.7	0.7	0.7	0.7
2 Value of (1) ($ billions, 1939 prices)	6.3	6.3	6.3	6.3	6.3
3 Earnings of those gainfully occupied in 1939, allowing for increased efficiency ($ billions, 1939 prices)	70.8	71.5	72.2	72.9	73.6
4 Increase per year in (3) ($ billions, 1939 prices)	0.7	0.7	0.7	0.7	0.7
5 Total increase ($ billions, 1939 prices) (2 + 4)	7.0	7.0	7.0	7.0	7.0
6 Index of resource prices	100	104	114	136	153
7 Total increase ($ billions, current prices) (5 x 6)/100	7.0	7.3	8.0	9.5	10.7
B SHORT TERM BASIS					
8 Income payments to individuals, 1939 resource prices (1st quarter, $ billions)	69.0	74.6	83.6	90.1	105.1
9 Increase per year ($ billions, 1939 prices)	5.6	9.0	6.5	15.0	2.9
10 Total increase ($ billions, current prices) (9 x 6)/100	5.6	9.4	7.4	20.4	4.4

LINE

1 Secular rate of additions to the gainfully occupied, based on average for 1919-38 (see Simon Kuznets, *National Income and Its Composition,* National Bureau of Economic Research, 1941, I, Table 8).

2 Line 1 multiplied by ($10,000 x $\frac{\$1,660}{\$1,839}$) or by $9,027. $10,000 is the value of net life earnings in 1923-28 prices estimated by J. M. Clark (*The Costs of the World War to the American People,* Yale University Press, 1931, pp. 217-8). $1,839 is the average payment per person engaged in 1923-28 (Kuznets, *op. cit.,* Tables 1 and 8); $1,660 is an estimate for 1939.

3 1939 entry, income payments to individuals, Department of Commerce estimate. For later years, entries are based on an annual growth of 1 per cent per gainfully occupied (slightly larger than the trend from 1909-18 to 1919-28; see *ibid.,* Table 11).

6 Table II 3.

8 For first quarter of 1939, income payments to individuals from *Survey of Current Business,* April 1944, p. 13, Table 9, line 1; extrapolated to other quarters by the movement of net national product in constant resource prices (App. Table II 12).

9 The entry for each year is the difference between its first quarter and the first quarter of the following calendar year. For 1943 the entry is the difference between its first and last quarters multiplied by 1⅓. For quarterly totals in 1939 prices see Appendix Table II 12.

their number, or of raising their productivity. Only the part of the flow of consumer goods that could be associated with the increase in the working population and its productivity, both viewed as potential contributions to war output, would be included in net national product.

A crude sample calculation for 1939-43 is given in Table I 4, in two variants. In the first, measuring the value of the secular rise in the working population and in its productivity, the long term addition to the gainfully occupied is valued at the average expected life earnings, in excess of the earner's own consumption needs; and the greater productivity of the population already working at the beginning of the period is based upon a crude secular rate per gainfully employed, total productivity being measured by income payments to individuals in constant prices.

This calculation disregards increases (or decreases) in the working population and its productivity in any single year. In the shorter term urgency of a war, it may be more appropriate to measure them, transient though they may be. For the important question is how much, during a given year, the economy has added to the gainfully occupied and to its productivity, an addition that may be available to expand war production in the few years of strain. Lines 8-10 of Table I 4 measure year-to-year increases in total 'deflated' earnings, i.e., in national product (in constant prices) attributable to producers.

If rises in the number of producers and in their productivity are net capital formation from the viewpoint of war output, so is net nonwar capital formation as ordinarily defined. Additions to stocks of commodities of various descriptions, or of claims, can be utilized to sustain a larger body of war producers in the future, if not directly for war production.

On the assumption that providing military goods is the sole purpose of economic activity, the first component of national product in order of logical priority is war output (Table I 5); in the same way as the first component in Table I 3 is the flow of goods to consumers. But total war output cannot be fully included in *net* national product, for not all items in it are finished goods from the standpoint of use in war. Munitions plants and construction units not in the theater of operations are in the nature of capital goods, and only net additions to them are to be included; hence the crude adjustments in passing from line 1 to line 3.[5]

TABLE I 5

Net National Product, on the Assumption of Provision of War Goods as the Sole Purpose, 1939-1943

(billions of dollars, current prices)

	1939	1940	1941	1942	1943
1 Gross war output	1.4	2.8	12.8	50.3	81.3
2 Depreciation on gov.-financed war construction	Negligible		0.3	0.8	1.8
3 Net war output (1 — 2)	1.4	2.8	12.5	49.5	79.5
4 Net capital formation, nonwar	(6.0)	(9.3)	(13.0)	(0.1)	(—6.5)
5 Value of increases in gainfully occupied and in their efficiency					
a) Based on Table I 4, line 7	(7.0)	(7.3)	(8.0)	(9.5)	(10.7)
b) Based on Table I 4, line 10	(5.6)	(9.4)	(7.4)	(20.4)	(4.4)
6 Net national product					
a) 3 + 4 + 5a	14.4	19.4	33.5	59.1	83.7
b) 3 + 4 + 5b	13.0	21.5	32.9	70.0	77.4

Lines 1-4 from Appendix Table II 11.

Parentheses in lines 4 and 5 signify that from the viewpoint of war use, the figures are to be adjusted by coefficients of unknown value. Lines 3, 4, and 5 are added (line 6) on the assumption that these coefficients equal 1 in all cases in all years.

The values customarily attached to net nonwar capital formation and net additions to the gainfully occupied and to its efficiency may not be the same as those that would be used were the goods included judged in terms of relevance to war production. What the adjustment coefficients, symbolized by the parentheses in lines 4 and 5, are, we do not know; but most probably they would be less than 1. The addition of the three components to a single national product total in Table I 5 is, therefore, quite arbitrary.

Yet the chief differences between this total and that in Table I 3 would remain regardless of any likely modifications of entries in Table I 5. In all years the national product totals in Table I 5

[5] One could draw the distinction even finer, and consider as finished only such war goods as reach the theaters of active combat (just as in consumers' outlay, in the customary approach, we measure finished goods when they enter the household). But it cannot be carried through statistically with the data commonly available.

would be smaller than in Table I 3, particularly before war output assumed its present dimensions. Also, in any transition from expenditures for defense alone to those for waging a major war, a national product total defined as in Table I 5 would rise much more relatively than the national product total in Table I 3 based, as it is, upon accepting the provision of consumer goods as the dominant goal of economic activity.

4 ASSUMPTION OF TWO END PURPOSES

For the transient period of a major war we might recognize two purposes coequal in primacy: provision of goods to consumers and for war use. The division of resources between the two would be arbitrary in that it would not be determined by a recognized and clear-cut principle within the framework of economic institutions. Were there such a principle (e.g., like that which establishes a relation between consumer goods and the capital equipment that produces them), it would so relate the two purposes as to indicate either the dominance of one or the subordinate position of both to some superior goal. That no such principle governs war and nonwar output seems fairly evident. While the proportion of resources to be devoted to a war is fixed by the urgencies of the military conflict up to a certain point, it is still a matter of choice, determined by conflicting pressures, political decisions, and judgments that attempt to arrive at a consensus by trial and error.

The assumption of two primary goals in wartime bears directly upon the statistical treatment of national product. Two categories of final products are measured at their gross value: goods flowing to individuals and households as ultimate consumers and goods flowing into the military conflict. Instead of one category of capital goods net additions to whose stock are included, the dichotomy of purposes means also a dichotomy in net additions to stocks of capital goods: nonwar and war net capital formation. There should, therefore, be at least four major product categories in a national product based on this assumption. In statistical practice, however, the flow of final war goods and war capital formation are lumped together in total war output (Table 1 6, Part A).

In Part B of Table I 6 national product is the sum of income

TABLE I 6

Net National Product, on the Assumption of Two Purposes:
To Provide Goods for Consumers and for the Military Conflict
1939-1943
(billions of dollars, current prices)

	1939	1940	1941	1942	1943
A FINAL PRODUCTS APPROACH					
1 Flow of goods to consumers	64.8	68.8	77.7	85.1	94.1
2 Net nonwar capital formation	6.0	9.3	13.0	0.1	—6.5
3 War output (excl. depreciation on war construction)	1.4	2.8	12.5	49.5	79.5
4 Net national product (1 + 2 + 3)	72.2	80.9	103.2	134.7	167.1
B PAYMENTS-SAVINGS APPROACH					
5 Income payments to individuals	70.8	76.2	92.7	116.6	142.3
6 Excess of contributions to social security over transfer payments	—0.4	—0.5	0.1	0.5	0.6
7 Net corporate savings, adj.	1.5	3.0	2.9	4.2	6.3
8 Additions to corporate income & profits taxes	0	0.3	1.6	6.0	11.2
9 Net business tax accruals	0.3	1.3	4.8	4.6	2.8
10 Depreciation on war construction	0	0	0.3	0.8	1.8
11 Adjustments for discrepancies	0	—0.4	—1.7	—0.6	1.2
12 Net national product (5 + 6 + 7 + 8 + 9 — 10 + 11)	72.2	79.9	100.1	130.5	162.6

LINE

1 & 2 Table I 3.

   3 Table I 5.

   5 *Survey of Current Business*, April 1944, p. 14, Table 12, line 5.

   6 *Ibid.*, p. 13, Table 12, lines 2 and 4.

   7 Adjusted for addition to 'other' business reserves, capital outlays charged to current expenses, and inventory revaluation (see *ibid.*, p. 13, Table 11, line 11, and p. 14, Table 13, lines 4, 5, and 6).

8 & 9 *Ibid.*, p. 10, Table B, line 2, and p. 11, Table 6, line 3.

  10 Table I 5.

  11 *Survey*, April 1944, p. 14, Table 13, line 7.

payments and savings.[6] In general, the gross value of war output

[6] National product as defined in either Section 2 or 3 cannot be estimated in this way, because the institutionally determined categories of income payments, business savings, and taxes do not (and cannot be made to) distinguish such items as consumption of war goods or ultimate consumption needed to sustain a constant body of producers at constant productivity. Even for the concept of national product in this section, the payment-savings approach cannot be used consistently as evidenced by the balancing adjustment needed to take account of depreciation on war construction (a relatively minor item).

must equal: (a) such part of the income payments to individuals as is not expended on the flow of consumer goods or on nonwar capital formation; (b) such part of net corporate savings (including additions to all reserve and accrual accounts) as is not expended on nonwar capital formation; (c) such part of business taxes as is not borne by income payments to individuals or expended for government services to business enterprises. In other words, the sum of the gross value of the flow of goods to consumers, net nonwar capital formation, and the gross value of war output should equal income payments to individuals, net corporate savings (as defined above), and such nonshiftable business taxes as go to pay for war output. The difficulty is in establishing the third item. However, it is reasonable to assume that corporate income and profits taxes, unlike other business taxes, are not shiftable to individuals' incomes; and that the increase in such taxes during a war is due primarily to the larger demands for funds occasioned by the expansion of war output. Accordingly, in line 8 of Table I 6, the increase in corporate income and profits taxes measures the part that may be assumed to finance *net* war output, and is adjusted for depreciation on war construction. The agreement between the two net national product totals is close (cf. lines 4 and 12).[7]

Obviously, national product totals based on the assumption of two goals must be larger than those based on one. If we accept a certain use for economic goods as a goal we must include their *full* value in national product; consequently, the more goals the more product categories included at their full gross value, and the larger the resulting total. The national product totals in Table I 6 are larger than those in Table I 3 by the amount of consumption deducted in Table I 3 to get net additions to stocks of war goods; larger than those in Table I 5 by the amount of the consumption of consumer goods allowed for in calculating the net accretion to the gainfully occupied and to its efficiency. Obviously were there a third purpose, *net* national product totals would be even larger than those in Table I 6.

[7] It is spurious in that the estimate of the flow of goods to consumers (line 1) is not independent of that of income payments to individuals (line 5). But an independent measure of the flow of goods to consumers, based on production and distribution data for the flow of final products, yields estimates that, while larger than those in line 1, would entail only minor (less than 5%) changes in national product.

5 NET AND GROSS

In a net national product total 'netness' does not mean that for all categories net additions are measured over and above current consumption. On the contrary, the chief and largest component is ordinarily the gross value of products flowing into such consumption as is considered the goal of economic activity; e.g., the full value of goods flowing to ultimate consumers. The distinction between net and gross national product is not, therefore, that the former allows for all consumption whereas the latter is gross of it in one or all categories. It is rather that gross national product is gross of consumption in some product categories that in net national product are measured net of such consumption because the goods are indirectly rather than directly for ultimate use.

Why is it useful to treat the output of such subsidiary goods on a gross basis, when only net additions to their stocks contribute to the goal of economic activity? Why, e.g., should we measure national product gross of the current consumption of durable capital, as is the practice in estimating peacetime gross national product?

Two reasons have customarily been adduced. The first rests on statistical expediency. Since to estimate accurately the current consumption of durable capital is difficult, and even the best estimate is subject to a wide margin of error, it is thought expedient to provide at least a total unaffected by the deduction of the statistically doubtful item, consumption of durable capital. This reason in itself is patently unacceptable. Were it the sole consideration, gross national product should be viewed as a statistical approximation to net national product, and, obviously, it would be a poor approximation. Some adjustment for current consumption is preferable, for it yields a smaller error than no adjustment.

But gross national product estimated according to peacetime definitions has a genuine *raison d'être*. For since in the short run, the economic life of durable capital is largely a matter of judgment, what constitutes a replacement of or an addition to durable capital is, for relatively brief periods, up to each entrepreneur. Thus, the very circumstance that makes estimating the current consumption of durable capital for a short period statistically hazardous makes entrepreneurial decisions to order production of such capital in the short run better understood when output is measured gross instead of net. Also, any relations between the flow of goods to consumers and capital formation that affect, in the short run, the composition of national product and perhaps the very changes in it, are, therefore, more apparent when capital formation (and hence national product) is measured gross of the current consumption of durable capital.[8]

This statement suggests the nature of the differences between net and gross national product concepts. The former, appraisals of the net contribution of economic activity to definite purposes, tend to disregard the fact that, in the short run, it may not be the net expected contribution that guides economic decisions. In the areas where economic activity or policy is geared in the short run to gross output, not to the net contribution to specific goals, net national product is modified into a gross national product concept. Net national product, based on continuously held goals, is both a short and a long term concept, although the difficulties inherent in measuring certain types of consumption for short periods carry over into measuring short term changes in net national product. Gross national product, by taking into account the fundamental economic mechanisms in their shorter range functioning, is essentially a short term concept. A long series of net national product totals has meaning as a set of cumulative and comparable figures. A long series of gross national product totals has meaning only as a string of figures for short term periods. In the longer run, consumption of durable capital must be deducted, since capital is physically destroyed or becomes obsolete beyond the point of any possible use. In the shorter run, it may be disregarded, since the shorter term choices, not being compelled by physical attrition or technical obsolescence, are better understood in terms of gross than of net capital formation. Differences among various concepts of *net* national product are reducible to differences in the goals with reference to which net contribution is measured, and in the ways the line is drawn between economic and noneconomic activities. Differences among various concepts of *gross* national product are, furthermore, determined by the category of products (and of corresponding activity) that are measured on a net addi-

[8] A similar argument applies to decisions of government as an entrepreneur with reference to the construction of war plants or housing. The reason for measuring national product gross of consumption of nonwar private durable capital is valid also for measuring it gross of consumption of public durable capital, war or nonwar.

tion basis in net national product, but are measured gross in gross national product (e.g., durable capital, government expenditures, or war production).

This distinction has direct bearing on the treatment of war output in estimating national product. So far as we study national product in the longer range, and view developments during a major war against this broader canvas, we gain nothing by using gross national product concepts. Only when we study wartime as a short term period do they become relevant. But even for such short terms the net national product concept of Section 3, based on providing military goods as the sole purpose of economic activity, has too little validity to warrant discussion. We devote ourselves to the concepts explained and illustrated statistically in Sections 2 and 4.

First, we consider treating durable capital on a gross rather than net basis. Whatever factors justify such treatment in peacetime would naturally affect years like 1939 through 1941, before war became a dominant drive in the country's economic activity. But even from the viewpoint of relevance to war needs, one may prefer to measure the *total* output of durable capital, i.e., not deduct current consumption. It is this total that measures the use of resources important in the war economy; and current consumption of durable capital is an unknown quantity in years of strain when all facilities, no matter how obsolete, are pressed into service. Therefore, for purposes of short term analysis, we measure national product gross of the consumption of durable capital in calculating both variants in Table I 7 (Part A, col. 2 and 3, and Part B, lines 5 and 6).

We next consider whether it is not also better in the shorter term run of a war to include the full value of all war output. The justification would not be that the provision of goods for the military conflict is an independent goal (as in Sec. 4). It would be rather that, given the long term meaning of war production as a capital cost, in the shorter run of a war social decisions are made with an eye to total war output; that economic activity is harnessed to programs that call for gross war output, not for net accretions to inventories of war goods. The reason is analogous to that for modifying net national product into a total gross of the consumption of durable capital; namely, in order to express it in the terms in which the immediate drives of economic activity are conceived.

TABLE I 7
Net and Gross National Product, the Several Variants Summarized
A OUTLINE OF COMPOSITION

NET NATIONAL PRODUCT (1)	ADD TO YIELD COL. 3 (2)	GROSS NATIONAL PRODUCT (Gross of durable capital consumption) (3)	ADD TO YIELD COL. 5 (4)	TOTALS GROSS OF DURABLE CAPITAL AND OF WAR GOODS CONSUMPTION (5)
		1 Peacetime Concept (war output as capital formation)		
Flow of goods to consumers		Flow of goods to consumers		Flow of goods to consumers
Net nonwar capital formation	Consumption of nonwar durable capital	Gross nonwar capital formation		Gross nonwar capital formation
Net additions to inventory of war goods & to war construction	Consumption of war construction	Net additions to inventory of war goods & gross additions to war construction	Consumption of war goods	Gross war output
		2 Wartime Concept (two end purposes)		
Flow of goods to consumers		Flow of goods to consumers		Flow of goods to consumers
Net nonwar capital formation	Consumption of nonwar durable capital	Gross nonwar capital formation		Gross nonwar capital formation
Net war output	Consumption of war construction	Gross war output		Gross war output

B APPROXIMATE TOTALS, 1939-1943
(billions of dollars, current prices)

	1939	1940	1941	1942	1943
Net National Product					
1 Variant 1, war output as capital formation	71.7	79.7	98.3	115.5	133.3
2 Variant 2, two end purposes	72.2	80.9	103.2	134.7	167.1
Consumption Items					
3 Consumption of durable capital, nonwar	7.2	7.4	7.9	8.7	9.2
4 Consumption of war construction	negligible	0.3	0.8	1.8	
Gross National Product (gross of consumption of durable capital)					
5 Variant 1 (1 + 3 + 4)	78.9	87.1	106.5	125.0	144.3
6 Variant 2 (2 + 3 + 4)	79.4	88.3	111.4	144.2	178.1
Totals Gross of Consumption of Durable Capital and of All War Goods					
7 Variant 1	79.4	88.3	111.4	144.2	178.1
8 Variant 2 (same as 6)	79.4	88.3	111.4	144.2	178.1

Line 1: Table I 3, line 4b; 2: Table I 6, line 4; 3 and 4: Table II 11; 7: sum of lines 1, 3, and consumption of war output (Table I 1, col. 1, minus Table I 2, col. 5).

As is inevitable, this total is identical with gross national product when two purposes are assumed and current consumption of durable capital is not deducted (Table I 7, Part A 1, col. 5, and Part A 2, col. 3, and Part B, lines 7 and 8). In the first, consumption of war goods is recognized in long term net analysis but disregarded in short term gross. In the second, the shorter term changes of war years are reflected in the very choice of goals; and hence the consumption of war goods would be disregarded even were the two purpose concept applied to a long period.

6 SUMMARY

For the uses estimates of national product serve, two interpretations of war production from the viewpoint of the purposes of economic activity seem preferable.

a) For short term studies a national product total that includes the full value of the flow of goods to consumers, gross nonwar capital formation, and the full value of war output seems most useful. The distinction between such wartime *gross* national product and *net* could be drawn along lines similar to those of peacetime, in that the latter would exclude the current consumption of durable capital (nonwar construction and equipment and war construction and industrial equipment). In other words, net national product would include the flow of goods to consumers, net nonwar capital formation, and war output net of the current consumption of war construction (see Table I 7, Part A 2, col. 1 and 3).

The wartime totals defined above differ from peacetime totals in that they include the value of war goods consumed. This difference is attributable to the assumption, for the short period associated with a major war, that economic activity has two purposes: provision of goods to consumers and for the armed conflict.

As indicated in Section 5, this wartime national product, gross of the consumption of durable capital, is statistically identical with a total computed by modifying the net national product concept of peacetime into a total gross of the consumption of both durable capital and *war goods* (see Table I 7, Part A 1, col. 5). The reason we consider it preferable to make the provision of goods for war a second purpose of economic activity and accordingly formulate wartime national product totals different from peacetime, on both a net and gross basis, stems from the need to emphasize the change a major war brings in the drives of economic activity. Even in a country that in peacetime devotes a substantial portion of its resources to war production, imminence of a major war entails a drastic reorientation of economic activity; and for the period associated with active participation, even the *net* contribution of economic activity cannot be judged solely from the viewpoint of providing goods to consumers or of any ultimate purpose other than that of helping the armed conflict. This break between peace and war years is even sharper in a country such as this, of whose resources only a minute proportion goes into war production in peacetime. To retain in a study of war years a net national product concept geared to the longer term dominance of pacific goals, and to take account of the war as a guiding purpose merely by coining a special gross product concept would leave the investigator open to the risk of minimizing the redirection of economic activity that occurs; and would yield net national product totals of small usefulness for such a short term study. To assure recognition of the cleavage in goals that occurs between peace- and wartime it seems better to admit the effect of a major war upon the very goals of economic activity in the short run, and give both net and gross national product wartime definitions.

b) For longer term studies net national product alone is relevant; and for it the treatment of war output as a species of capital formation seems to be the sole appropriate approach. Once our assumption that the purpose of economic activity is to provide goods to consumers is accepted, war output can have meaning only as capital formation designed to maintain or increase the flow within an institutional framework that does not preclude war as an instrument of national policy.

If war output is interpreted in this way, the difference between the resulting estimates of net national product and national income as estimated in this country in the past depends upon which method of measuring income originating in government activity and the consumption of war goods (see Sec. 2) is chosen. If income originating in government is measured on a payment basis, i.e., net government savings are taken into account, the implied calculation of additions to government assets (to be used as an offset against an increase in government debt) should include also additions to the inventory of war goods. If it is measured on a cost basis, national product should be adjusted to take account of net investment or disinvestment on war account.

In both treatments of income originating in government activity, the effect of the adjustment for the consumption of war goods will be marked only during a major war and the years immediately following, for only then will the stock of war goods subject to depreciation be large. In other years the adjustment for net investment or disinvestment on war account can be merely a minor fraction of net national product.

In conclusion, we stress the dependence of the concept and the estimates upon the definition of the purpose of economic activity. National product cannot be measured for the years of a major war as it is in peacetime because the customary long run assumptions concerning the goals of economic activity are not basic. Is provision of goods to ultimate consumers in fact the sole purpose that guides and should be used to evaluate economic activity? When the very life of a social system is at stake the everyday purposes of economic activity are overshadowed. Yet since from the *longer run* viewpoint they are dominant, we retain the peacetime goal—provision of goods to consumers.

This goal is not always dominant. In other countries, in other times, even from a long term viewpoint, provision of goods to consumers may not be or have been the sole purpose of economic activity. For example, where the basic consideration in the longer run—three or four decades—is to build up capital in order to hasten industrialization and come abreast of more advanced countries, a longer term goal is perhaps better defined as to provide goods for capital accumulation; then the net contribution of economic activity should be measured in terms of net capital formation as ordinarily defined plus additions to the productive population and to its efficiency. Still other countries may well reach a stage when the maximization of economic goods for the benefit of ultimate consumers is not the dominant goal, unless under economic goods we include leisure or participation in activities which we may put under the heading of the fine arts. At this later stage the full economic potential may perhaps not be exploited to provide goods to consumers; and economic activity proper may be reduced to afford more opportunity for noneconomic pursuits. Under such conditions the net contribution of economic activity would be measured in terms of the net balance of consumer goods over their cost, the latter treated as a draft on such desirable ends as greater leisure for noneconomic pursuits.

From many viewpoints, the provision of goods to consumers is a subsidiary rather than a primary aim of economic activity. If the functioning of the economic system is judged by its contribution to social welfare at large, if some idea of a good life is the touch-stone, then both provision of goods to consumers and any other immediate purpose of economic activity will be subordinate, and the entire calculation of national product, if calculation is still possible, will be different. No longer an economic concept, national product will become a concept within a broader frame of reference. If the social philosophy of recent years, which minimizes the system of values inherent in economic institutions and tends to subordinate it to some idea of a good life, of national glory, or of some other nebulous criterion deemed superior, is adopted, the net contribution of economic activity will have to be measured on the basis of the new and extra-economic goals. The customary measures of national product assume not only the end purposes that guide economic activity but also that they are within the economic framework proper and are independent of goals that, however superior, are not reflected in economic institutions in their day to day operation.

APPENDIX I

Comparison with Department of Commerce Concepts

The wartime concepts of net and gross national product defined in the text (Table I 7, Part A 2) differ not only from the longer term peace-time concepts, but also from those currently used by the Department of Commerce. As estimated by the Department of Commerce, national income is the sum of income payments (including savings of individual entrepreneurs) and of undistributed corporate profits net of taxes, i.e., it is defined statistically as it was in peacetime. But whereas in peacetime a total so measured closely approximates net national product—the value of all final goods and of additions to the stock of capital (fixed, working, and claims against foreign countries)—

it does not in wartime. Besides the flow of consumer goods and additions to stocks of capital goods of the usual type, it includes a substantial portion, but only a portion, of war output (specifically, that financed out of direct personal taxes, individuals' savings, and corporate savings). Consequently, whatever significance can still be attributed to it as an estimate of the flow of the means of payments to individuals and accretions to freely disposable funds of corporations,[9] it is no longer net national product.

We have defined the latter for wartime as the sum of the flow of goods to consumers, net nonwar capital formation, and war output net of depreciation on war construction. On a payment level, this total would be approximated by adding to income payments and undistributed corporate profits (net of depreciation and taxes) the increase in corporate taxes and tax accruals (adjusted for depreciation on war construction, see Table I 6). The latter is the amount by which net national product, as defined by us, exceeds national income as currently measured by the Department.

'Gross national product at market prices' rather than national income is the concept the Department of Commerce uses as a comprehensive total of which war output could properly be treated as a component. On the product level, it is the sum of the flow of goods to consumers (excluding direct government services), private gross capital formation, and all goods flowing to government (government expenditures on goods and services). On the payments-savings level, it equals national income plus all business taxes.[10]

Two arguments are adduced by the Department in explaining its introduction of 'gross national product at market prices'. The first is the need for a total that would yield a correct estimate of consumers' outlay after 'war expenditures and any other nonconsumer

[9] If the main purpose is to gauge the flow of disposable funds to individuals and corporations, one may argue that a more suitable total would be of income payments to individuals net of direct personal taxes, plus undistributed corporate profits net of *all* taxes.

[10] This description disregards the adjustments made by the Department in estimating corporate profits, since they would be proper also to a peacetime concept of gross national product.

For a discussion of the concept and the reasons for its adoption, see Milton Gilbert: 'Measuring National Income as Affected by the War', *Journal of the American Statistical Association*, June 1942, pp. 186-98; also the several articles presenting the estimates in various issues of the *Survey of Current Business* since 1942, especially the first, in the March 1942 issue.

spending' have been deducted. The second is that the total covers all finished products at market prices rather than at factor cost.

Both arguments would be as valid for our wartime concepts of national product. If subtraction of *war* expenditures and other nonconsumer purchasing (i.e., presumably nonwar capital formation) is to leave a residual that properly measures consumers' outlay, then the total should be a sum of consumers' outlay, capital formation, and *war* expenditures (gross or net of depreciation on war construction). But, in general, this 'subtraction' argument is not relevant unless it indicates the reason why a given type of outlay is to be treated as a subtrahend from a comprehensively defined minuend of national product. If the reason is that war output measures *final* products, and should, therefore, be included in national product in the same way as the flow of consumer goods is, then the total would be estimated as described in the text. It would have to include all government outlays only on the implicit assumption that all are for final products.[11]

The second argument, which contrasts measurement at factor cost and at market prices, is relevant only if government outlays are to be kept as a separate category of national product. If, however, we are free to allocate national product by categories, either the peacetime or the wartime concepts defined in the text can be interpreted as totals in market prices. For example, net national product in peacetime is the sum of (a) flow of goods to consumers at market prices; (b) private net capital formation at market prices; (c) public net capital formation at market or cost prices. And, both net and gross national product, wartime concept, are sums of (a) flow of goods to consumers; (b) nonwar capital formation, private and public; (c) goods purchased by government for war purposes, all at market prices. The Department's gross national product differs from other totals only in that it includes the entire government outlay on goods at market prices; the other totals include only the portion not already covered under the market values of products of the private business system. The crucial difference is in the treatment of *all* government activity as a congeries of final products; not in the evaluation at market price rather than factor cost.

This is not to be taken as implying that gross national product, as defined by the Department, does not have its uses and a mean-

[11] Or for a different theoretical reason discussed below.

ing. Providing the main argument for it, they lie in the implicit assumption of government outlay as an independent variable that can be modified directly by public policy. This independent variable is then conceived to be of telling effect on national product as a dependent variable.[12]

Such an assumption is inherent in the general line of reasoning that leads to estimating national product gross as well as net. When theoretical or empirical considerations require the assumption that changes in the total product of the economic system or alternative policy steps are better understood if a given activity is measured gross rather than net, there is argument for measuring it gross and for making national product correspondingly gross. What is in the part must also be in the whole.

The difficulty in defining a comprehensive gross national product total is that its size depends upon the character of the industrial classification: the more industrial divisions distinguished the larger it would be because of the greater duplication caused by repeated counting of products of one industry consumed by another. In this sense, there is no such thing as a uniquely determined gross national product.

This difficulty may be avoided by a second approach. To make the part and the whole comparable, we can, upon treating all government outlay on goods and services as if it were for finished goods, include it fully with the two other chief components of finished output—consumer goods flowing to households and individuals (excluding government services) and private gross capital formation. This is the gross national product total of the Department of Commerce. It is measured gross with respect to activities in two areas: private capital formation and government activities of all descriptions. The distinctive feature lies in treating government activity on a gross basis.

Were we for some reason to consider the activity of the steel industry, rather than of government, paramount in determining national product or policy, national product would be measured gross of the consumption of (a) durable capital outside the steel industry; (b)

[12] Presumably not directly, but indirectly, in the way government expenditures are financed, and hence modified to measure income-creating activities of the government. However, at the first stage of analysis, *all* government outlays, and a national product total that would include them fully, must be considered.

the steel industry's product, i.e., the part of the industry's purchases of commodities and services that is covered in the value of consumers' outlay and in gross capital formation outside the steel industry. In other words, we measure gross only the contribution of the particular industry whose total outlay is considered a proper measure of its activity. The meaning of such a gross national product obviously depends upon the propriety of emphasizing the gross value of a given industry's activity, and accordingly of treating it as if it were for finished products. In the case of government activity, the meaning depends upon the validity of an assumption that, in essence, makes government outlay an important independent variable in determining the total product of the nation.[13]

If the above argument is valid, two further comments are in order. First, so far as the assumption concerning the importance of government outlay is valid for postwar years, gross national product, as defined by the Department of Commerce, will continue to be useful. It is not a purely wartime concept but rather one inherent in a certain view of the role of government activity.

Second, like all gross totals, it does not measure the *net* contribution of economic activity properly. Before it can tell us what economic activity contributes to the satisfaction of the ends society pursues it must be freed from the duplication that, by definition, it contains. Useful as it may be as a step in an analysis that may serve to relate public policy and net economic output, it is only an intermediate step that must be followed by others before the ultimate effects of public policy can be assayed.

[13] This and the preceding two paragraphs follow closely the author's discussion in 'Taxes and National Income', *Proceedings of the American Philosophical Society*, Feb. 1944.

PART II

National Product, 1939-1943

The discussion in this Part follows closely the text of *Occasional Paper 17*, 'National Product, War and Prewar' (National Bureau of Economic Research, Feb. 1944). Changes have been made to take account of the more recent estimates of the Department of Commerce, and to bring the series through the last two quarters of 1943.

For a critical review of the *Occasional Paper* and a discussion of the methods used see *Review of Economic Statistics*, Vol. XXVI, No. 3, August 1944, pp. 109-35.

1 National Product in Current Prices

As defined in Part I, national product in wartime is the sum of finished output: (a) flow of goods to ultimate consumers; (b) additions to the stock of nonwar capital; (c) flow of goods to war uses; (d) additions to the stock of war capital. Components (a) and (b) constitute nonwar output, the nonwar sector; components (c) and (d), war output, the war sector. National product is net or gross as components (b) and (d) are measured net or gross of the current consumption of durable capital.

The estimates in Table II 1 are merely approximations to national product so defined because the data are not sufficiently detailed to measure accurately final product categories. The following comments serve to indicate the respects in which the estimates fail to give what is wanted.

The value of goods flowing to, or retained from their production by households and individuals (line 1) excludes subsistence and related expenditures by the government for the armed forces. Theoretically, it should include them, since it should measure all goods flowing to consumers qua consumers. There is no more reason to exclude the value of subsistence for the armed services from the flow of consumer goods (as a measure of a distinct category of final products) because it is covered in war output than to exclude expenditures on consumer goods by workers in munitions plants. The subsistence item under war output, together with pay, is the value of services rendered by the military forces; and there is no duplication if the goods are treated also as part of the flow of goods to ultimate consumers.

This item is not easy to measure. It should include only the part of the allowance for food, clothing, shelter, etc. that is a minimum needed by the armed forces as peacetime consumers; not the part that represents special needs arising from the particular demands of military activity. Yet to say what part of total expenditures on food, clothing, shelter, transportation, etc. for the armed forces is equivalent to a peacetime consumption minimum and what part is due to special military needs is difficult. It may be argued that since the value of the services of the armed forces is determined arbitrarily, a simpler method would be to equate it to money payments alone, thereby allowing in war output for the flow of consumer goods to members of the armed forces qua ultimate consumers. But this would seriously undervalue the services of the armed forces, calling for a subsequent correction, and mis-classify under war output a portion of the flow of goods to consumers. It was deemed preferable to characterize the omission as a qualification upon our estimates of the flow of consumer goods. Could this item be included, both the flow of goods to consumers and national product in a year like 1942 would be $2 to $3 billion larger than the totals in Table II 1.[1]

TABLE II 1

National Product, Wartime Concept, Current Prices
1939-1943
(billions of dollars)

	1939	1940	1941	1942	1943
1 Flow of goods to consumers	64.8	68.8	77.7	85.1	94.1
2 Nonwar capital formation					
a) Gross	13.2	16.7	20.9	8.8	2.7
b) Net	6.0	9.3	13.0	0.1	—6.5
3 War output					
a) Gross	1.4	2.8	12.8	50.3	81.3
b) Net	1.4	2.8	12.5	49.5	79.5
4 National product					
a) Gross (1 + 2a + 3a)	79.4	88.3	111.4	144.2	178.1
b) Net (1 + 2b + 3b)	72.2	80.9	103.2	134.7	167.1

For derivation see Appendix II and Appendix Table II 11. Since these estimates use the recent work of the Department of Commerce, the coverage of the components is not the same as that in National Bureau estimates. The two chief differences are (a) flow of goods to consumers excludes imputed rent on owner-occupied houses; (b) net private capital formation, the major part of total nonwar capital formation, is the residual left after subtracting depreciation and depletion as recorded in business accounts, i.e., unadjusted to current reproduction value. Also, viewed as sums of income payments and undistributed savings of enterprises, the totals implicitly disregard government savings, i.e., set them at zero.

The value of services to individuals by governments in peacetime is assumed, somewhat arbitrarily, to be equal to direct personal taxes paid by individuals. There is no reason to modify the assumption in wartime: at least prewar direct tax payments may be interpreted as compensation for services by governments to individuals, and only the increase in direct taxes attributed to the additional

[1] If we assume minimum subsistence to be $500 per member of the armed forces, and 4 million in the armed forces in 1942, the item amounts to $2 billion. It would tend to rise rapidly from 1941 to 1943, accentuating the rise shown in Table II 1.

services rendered in war. For this reason, prewar direct taxes are added to round out consumers' expenditures to total outlay.[2]

Before we can estimate nonwar capital formation (line 2) we have to differentiate war from nonwar capital goods. Some part of the addition to privately financed equipment and construction was, during the years covered in Table II 1, specifically designed for the production of war implements or their components; and a substantial proportion of both private and public nonwar capital formation, while not directly associated with munitions production, was due to the expansion of activity associated with the war. In a sense, all capital formation in a period of intensive preparation for or participation in a major war is for military purposes, stimulated in the short run by war needs.

Yet the classification cannot be based upon purposes—for they are intangible. It should rather take into account the extent to which equipment and construction are either of such physical character as to be suitable only for war production in the narrowest sense or of such extraordinary size as can be warranted by war demands alone and in no way be justified by reasonable estimates of peacetime needs. As this cannot be done with the present data, the best practicable criterion is the source of financing. Additions to capital equipment that are specifically for transient war needs and are so unwarranted by peacetime prospects as to require government financing could be defined as capital formation for war purposes. Private financing or government financing outside the war budget was considered evidence that the capital formation involved could be defined as nonwar in the longer run.

War output in line 3 differs from the usual estimate of war expenditures in excluding payments that do not represent a draft upon real resources (property purchase, prepayments, and the like); and in line 3b, in excluding also depreciation on government-financed war construction and equipment. Neither adjustment can be statistically precise.

[2] It may be argued that a more reasonable method would be to allow for an increase in direct taxes associated with the rising cost per unit of governmental services. This correction, however, would be for a relatively small part of the total, and would call for a subsequent adjustment of the totals in current prices by a price index for governmental services. In calculating totals in 1939 prices, direct taxes were held constant at the 1939 price level, the assumption being that the real volume of services to consumers did not change.

Another disadvantage of the estimates in line 3 is that part of war output is measured before it reaches the units that dispose of it for purposes of the armed conflict. Even in the series for munitions, products accepted by the military agencies and ready for combat or training use are combined with products subject to further modification. While there is no duplication, war output is not as truly a finished products total as the flow of consumer goods.[3]

The above qualifications stem from a single cause: the available information is on categories of outlay by source, a not unambiguous guide to the categories of final products. Yet the disparities between what we wish and can measure are not sufficient to preclude analysis.

Table II 1 reveals marked changes in national product and in its composition: a striking increase in the total in current prices from 1939 to 1943; a spectacular climb of war output to high proportions of national product; an increase in nonwar capital formation until 1941, then a drastic contraction; an impressive increase in consumers' expenditures, retarded after 1941.

However, there is little purpose in analyzing here the estimates in current prices. Our interest is in real output and the relative proportions of its components measured in real terms; and for this purpose Table II 1 may be quite misleading. Even in peacetime, values in current prices tend to disguise movements in real output and contain some elements of noncomparability in the price structure and in the price fluctuations of national product components. But in peacetime these elements of noncomparability and heterogeneity are few because price changes and shifts are usually not violent. In wartime, however, prices tend to fluctuate violently and bases of valuation for the war and nonwar sectors of the economy are inherently noncomparable. Estimates in current prices are then merely a first step toward estimates of national product and its components in real terms. The next step is obviously to measure price changes and differentials.

2 PRICE CHANGES AND DIFFERENTIALS: THE PROBLEM

The national product totals given above are sums of final products, each valued at changing price levels and on bases possibly differ-

---

[3] On the other hand, additions to inventories held by the government on war account and not yet paid for are omitted. To this extent, the total understates the increase in war output, at least when it is expanding.

ent from one component to another. To make these totals internally consistent and unaffected by temporal changes in prices we need indexes designed to adjust values in current prices for both price changes and differentials.

We assume first that the valuation base current in recent prewar years for nonwar goods is appropriate for estimating national product in real terms comparable as between war- and peacetime. The alternative would be to accept the valuation base for the war sector in wartime and try to modify the base for the nonwar sectors; in other words, to value each component of national product just as war goods are valued. Obviously it would be difficult to translate all components of national product to the unusual and rapidly shifting valuation base that determines the pricing of war goods. Even if it were not, national product totals covering *both* peace- and wartime would be more comparable and internally consistent if based on peacetime valuations, for not only are they more persistent in the longer run but also constitute a more familiar set of values for appraising changes in wartime.[4]

If this position is conceded, the task in the nonwar sector is solely to find reliable measures of changes in prices over time. Formidable difficulties arise even here. Price indexes do not reflect fully qualitative deterioration in commodities and services; the 'pricing up' that takes the form of adding superficial and unwanted elements to the good, largely in order to raise it into higher price brackets without violating price regulations; the reduction in discounts or in services formerly granted in connection with durable commodities; pricing on black markets; and the general effects of a narrowing freedom of choice on the part of would-be civilian purchasers. As indicated in Section 3, only a few halting steps can be taken toward overcoming these difficulties. Still for the nonwar sector we can construct indexes of final product prices that, when applied to totals in current prices, yield approximate estimates of the relevant components of national product at prewar market prices.

The war sector presents more serious difficulties. To begin with, prices of final products (various items of munitions and of war construction) are not freely accessible; nor are they in existence during the full period spanning both prewar and war years, for many

4 With the conclusion of the war, new nonwar bases may be used, preferably of a postwar year relatively free from the disturbing effects of war.

of the items were not produced until this country got well into the war. Even when items produced in 1939-40 and 1942-43 are superficially similar, e.g., war planes, certain types of guns, and merchant ships, the qualitative change is such that the resemblance is more in name than in substance. It is impossible to construct directly a price index of war products that would span both prewar and war years.

Even were it possible, price and valuation bases for the war and nonwar sectors would still not be comparable; or, following the preference just indicated, it would still be necessary to adjust prices of war products to a valuation base comparable with that which determines prices of peacetime goods on the free markets of the economy. Commodities and services for use in the armed conflict are purchased under conditions radically different from those that govern transactions in peace type products on the market. Hence, even if we expressed war output as totals in constant prices of munitions, war construction, and nonmunitions, the valuation of at least the first two components would be quite different from that of peacetime goods; and we would be adding into national product physical quantities multiplied by a heterogeneous set of weights.

It may be argued that the rather lavish use of monetary incentives and of laws and regulations, which condition the prices of war products in wartime, represents a shift in consumer preferences on a par with changes in more normal times; or that it is a mere quantitative expansion of the area of governmental purchasing and government-destined production, which in peacetime also is characterized by valuation practices substantially different from those in private markets. To the first argument one may reply that if there are such violent and drastic shifts in consumer preference, estimates of national product cease to have any meaning unless based on a relatively fixed set of values that consciously ignore such shifts. A reply to the second argument is that while government-bound production and products of the private business system are not valued on comparable bases in peacetime, the former is so small in years of peace that the distortion in the national product totals is negligible; but that the matter cannot be dismissed so lightly when the government-controlled sector becomes as large as it does during a major war.[5] At any rate, it seemed better to

[5] If after this war the scope of government-controlled activity extends and continues

wrestle with the problem than ignore it or reduce it to a question of temporal changes only in final product prices in the war sector.

We attempt therefore to value war output not at actual 1939 prices (if such could be found), but at prices it would have fetched in 1939 had it been produced under conditions comparable to peacetime, i.e., when producers could attain the efficiency of resource input characteristic of comparable peacetime industries grown to maturity without the haste and waste of wartime. The concept may seem unrealistic; but it is only so far as any application of peacetime criteria to wartime is unrealistic. And if we are to have national product totals continuous and comparable as between prewar and war years, and some basis for evaluating war output in its longer range postwar aspect, we cannot avoid introducing arbitrarily a common base.

In this attempt we must begin with evaluation at the resource input level. At the final products level there is no comparability between peacetime goods and war implements. The choice between butter and machine guns is not made in the way consumers' demand determines the choice between bread and cake; nor is the government in the position of a producer who chooses among capital goods according to his knowledge or anticipation of consumers' demand. But resources common to both butter and machine guns can be identified; and some can be specifically tagged as having been used to produce the former in peacetime and the latter in wartime. It is thus at the resource input level that the first step can be taken to reduce elements of heterogeneity (at a point of time) and of noncomparability (over time) in wartime national product in current prices.

The element of *heterogeneity* is this: identical or comparable resources utilized at a given time for different ends (e.g., civilian and war goods) are not compensated at the same monetary rates, but the differences in compensation do not correspond to differences in the efficiency of use. The elements of *noncomparability* (over time) are two: (i) identical or comparable resources in identical or comparable uses at two different points of time are not com-

to be conditioned by rules quite different from those of the private market place, the problem will remain formidable and will require careful reconsideration of the somewhat arbitrary compromises made in estimating national product for this country before this war.

pensated at the same monetary rates; (ii) identical or comparable resources shifting over time to different uses (e.g., from peace to war production) are not compensated at the same monetary rates, but the differences in compensation do not correspond to differences in efficiency of use.

Therefore measuring war (and hence total) output in real terms raises two distinct questions: What changes occur over time in the monetary compensation of identical or comparable resources? Does a change from peace to war production mean that identical or comparable units of productive resources are used more or less efficiently? The separation of the two elements of noncomparability is artificial in that the resources that shift to new uses undergo changes both in monetary compensation per efficiency unit and in efficiency. But it is easier to measure them separately, and as the first is obviously much more susceptible of definition and measurement, it is treated first.

The successive steps are: (i) To measure changes over time in final product prices for consumer goods, nonwar capital formation, and certain components of war output (nonmunitions) (Sec. 3a). (ii) To measure changes in prices of resources entering the major part of war output (munitions and war construction) (Sec. 3a). (iii) To assume changes in the efficiency of resource input in the nonwar sectors and nonmunitions, then convert the indexes under (i) to indexes of the compensation of resources, with which we can translate national product and its components to resource input at 1939 prices (Sec. 3b). (iv) To assume changes in and the relative levels of the efficiency of resource input in munitions and war construction, then convert the indexes under (ii) to indexes of the final product prices of munitions and war construction, i.e., prices on a base identical with peacetime prices of products of comparable industries. Once the price differentials between peace and war goods have been eliminated, national product and its components can be translated to a consistent level of final output in 1939 prices (Sec. 3c).

3   Price Changes and Differentials: Procedures and Assumptions

a Price indexes for products and resources

The degree to which price and other data can be made to reflect quality and quantity changes in the nonwar sector, and differences in the productivity of resources between the nonwar and war sectors, determines the degree of our success in measuring national product and its components in real terms. The procedures are described in detail in Appendix II, but the estimates cannot be understood without some introduction here.

To test the adequacy of the price indexes used by the Department of Commerce to translate consumers' outlay into constant prices, we compared movements in 'deflated' totals with changes in output destined for civilian use. This test, applied to food products and apparel (clothing and shoes), seemed to warrant a substantial correction for the understatement of the price indexes (for this particular purpose). In all other commodity groups and for some sectors of the service group, the price data customarily used, which are commonly acknowledged to reflect inadequately the types of price change briefly indicated in the opening paragraphs of Section 2, could not be adjusted. Consequently, even our overall price indexes for the flow of goods to consumers may understate the price rise; if so, the price adjusted totals overstate the increase or understate the decline in the 'real' value of the flow of goods to consumers.[6]

Since the Department of Commerce price indexes for nonwar capital formation represent the most practicably complete utilization of available data on the prices of final products, they were used. Here too restrictions and smaller supply have led to quality de-

---

[6] An adjustment made in *Occasional Paper 17* to re-weight the various price indexes for services has now been carried through by the Department of Commerce, and we have used their recent price indexes for this category.

No great accuracy is claimed for the correction made in the price indexes for food and clothing. Indeed it may well overstate the price rise in these two categories. But if so, the overstatement may serve to offset the downward bias in the price indexes for the other commodity and service groups. And the price measures wanted here—indexes of changes in costs of commodities and services to all consumers, reflecting shifts in their residence and employment status as well as the full complex of changes in the quality of goods—are quite different from such measures as the BLS cost of living index, which reflects changes only in the prices paid by a settled group of wage earners and low-salaried employees.

terioration, reduction of discounts and services customary in more normal times, and a narrowing of the would-be buyer's choice. There is, therefore, ground for assuming that the indexes understate the price rise, and that, consequently, the totals adjusted for price changes overstate values in constant prices.

Under war output 'nonmunitions' and 'munitions and war construction' were estimated separately. The former comprise military pay and subsistence allowances; salaries of civilians in war agencies; subsistence outlays as well as travel for the armed forces; agricultural exports to allies; and similar miscellaneous items. The price indexes for the commodity items were based on Bureau of Labor Statistics wholesale price data; for the pay items, on known changes in rates of pay. Though rather crude, they contain no perceptible biases.

'Munitions and war construction' are dominated by items of specific use in the armed conflict and subject to the rapid qualitative changes associated with active warfare—planes, guns, ammunition, naval ships, merchant ships, war construction units (barracks, depots, airfields, etc., government-financed war plants and war housing). The price indexes, based on the compensation of resources rather than on the prices of final products, were built up from separate indexes for the three resource categories: labor costs; gross profits, allocable between returns to capital and enterprise; and corporate income and excess profits taxes. The weights assigned to these three resource cost indexes (the price adjustment was made separately for the three subtotals, each representing the relevant cost category) were based on the division of the gross value product in the five 'war' industries (metal mining, oil and gas mining, metals fabrication, chemicals and petroleum refining in manufacturing, and contract construction) that accounted for the bulk of munitions output and war construction in 1942 and 1943.

The price measure for the labor factor is an index of hourly earnings in 44 war manufacturing industries weighted by current year man hours. The total current cost of the capital and enterprise factor was calculated by multiplying the total value of munitions and war construction by the changing ratio of the combined total of corporate net income after taxes, depreciation, entrepreneurial income, interest, and net rents and royalties to the gross value product of the five 'war' industries. The corresponding price measure was obtained by dividing an index (1939=100) of the total value of these items in the five 'war' industries by an index of the consumption of raw materials of mineral origin. The latter, prepared by G. H. Moore, was taken to measure changes in the physical volume of capital and enterprise input. Finally, it was assumed that the corporate taxes (income and excess profits) paid in 1939 were the monetary equivalent of the government's contribution to business activity, and that, after 1939, such services increased with real output, i.e., with deflated labor, capital, and enterprise costs. Accordingly, the deflated totals of labor, capital, and enterprise costs were multiplied by the ratio of 1939 taxes in the five 'war' industries to the 1939 total of such costs; the result measures governmental services (at 1939 prices) rendered in connection with these activities.

Of course the assumptions adopted to construct price indexes for the various categories of resources embodied in munitions and war construction can easily be challenged. Attempts to attach quantities to processes whose substantive scope is exceedingly difficult to ascertain, the indexes are submitted here in the realization that fuller data may make better estimates possible in the future. But crude as the indexes are as measures of changes in compensation per resource unit entering munitions and war construction, the implicit assumptions are, on the whole, in the direction of under- rather than overstating the rise in resource prices. For both labor and the human part of capital and enterprise the procedure assumes that the groups involved are comparable through the years with respect to skill and training. But this means that the price indexes neglect the dilution of skill and experience in labor and managerial groups.[7] Furthermore, for both labor and nonlabor factors, the procedure assumes that in each industry covered, compensation of factors engaged in war production has increased since 1939 at the same rate as compensation of factors engaged in the same industry in all work. That is, the indexes neglect the possibly greater increase by 1942 or 1943 in the pay to factors engaged in war production proper

[7] There is an offsetting factor in the undervaluation of the services of the armed forces and war agency personnel included under nonmunitions. The relative magnitudes cannot be gauged; but there is some doubt that the underpayment of the armed forces and war agency personnel relative to their potential earnings is equal to or greater than the overpayment of labor or management in war production relative to their skills and training by prewar standards.

than in the compensation of factors still engaged in the same industries in peace type work.

True, there are offsets that might reduce the downward bias of the price indexes. The index of earnings per man hour covers wage earners in selected industries that by 1942 may have been engaged chiefly in war work. It is quite possible that price per unit of input of other labor entering war outlay (salaries in war industries, payments to employees in transportation or other fields serving the war but not covered in our index) may have risen less from 1939 to 1942 than earnings per man hour in the 44 manufacturing industries. Similarly, compensation of nonlabor factors, entering war output but not covered in our indexes, may have risen less than is indicated. However, a rough balancing of these considerations, which can be nothing but a guess, would suggest that the offsets would not fully cancel the downward bias of the price indexes. Consequently, like the price indexes for other components of national product, and perhaps to an even greater degree, the indexes of compensation of productive factors entering war output may understate the price rise between 1939 and 1943.

Prices of goods to consumers rose more in 1942 and 1943 according to the index in Table II 2, line 1, than according to the customary cost of living index (line 5). As indicated in Appendix II, Section 1, some of the difference may be due to an improperly full imputation of our adjustments in food and clothing to the price indexes. Perhaps some should be attributed to a bias in the current price totals. But the greater proportion is due to the emphasis in

TABLE II 2

Final Product and Resource Price Indexes
National Product Components, 1939-1943
1939 = 100

Price Indexes for	1939	1940	1941	1942	1943
1 Flow of goods to consumers (excl. gov. services)	100	101	107	122	134
2 Nonwar construction & equipment, gross	100	101	107	116	123
3 War output, gross	100	112	128	144	160
4 Wholesale prices, BLS	100	102	113	128	134
5 Cost of living, BLS	100	101	106	117	124

The indexes in lines 1-3 are implicit: totals in current prices divided by the corresponding totals in 1939 prices. For a detailed description of the procedures and the quarterly and annual totals see Appendix II.

the BLS index on measuring price changes of a relatively constant bundle of goods going to a settled body of wage earning and low-salaried families. The indexes appropriate for the 'deflation' of consumers' outlay should reflect also the effects of migration; quality deterioration, even though not compensable by larger money outlay; and changes in the cost of living of consumer groups other than those covered by the BLS index.

The rise in prices of resources entering war output was relatively sharp (line 3). Since the index covers also prices (at the final product level) of nonmunitions, which rose less, the rate of compensation of resources associated with munitions and war construction proper rose even more than is indicated in line 3.

Table II 2 brings us to an intermediate stage in the analysis. The indexes in lines 1 and 2 (and part of that in line 3) are for prices of final products; those dominating the entries in line 3, for prices of resources. Were we to apply these indexes in adjusting the relevant components of national product, one part of the latter would represent a sum of final products at their 1939 prices; the other, a sum of productive resources at their 1939 prices. The two parts can legitimately be added only by one of two further steps: (1) estimate changes in the efficiency of resources in the area outside munitions and war construction, then convert the final product price indexes into measures of changes in the compensation of resources at their 1939 efficiency level; in which case the national product totals, when adjusted for price changes, become consistent measures of the 'real' value of resource input at a constant efficiency level; or (2) estimate changes after 1939 in the efficiency of resources put into munitions and war construction; then convert the totals for munitions and war construction into measures of final output, comparable with the other components of national product.

b *Conversion to resource prices*

The few scattered data on the efficiency of resources in the nonwar sector (chiefly in some manufacturing and mining industries and utilities on a per man hour base) suggest that the rise since 1939 has been moderate, at an annual rate of not more than 2 or 3 per cent; that it virtually ceased by 1942; and that in recent quarters, as the scale of operations in many civilian industries shrank and dilution of labor and other resources took place, efficiency per resource unit may have declined slightly.

On the basis of such meager evidence, a quarterly efficiency index was constructed and applied uniformly to the price indexes (at final product prices) for three of the chief components of national product (flow of consumer goods, excluding direct taxes; nonwar construction and equipment; the nonmunitions part of war output). The price indexes for final products were thereby converted into price indexes for resources in terms of their efficiency in 1939.[8]

Even if this single efficiency index is accurate, its application to such different groups of final products as are represented by consumers' outlay, nonwar construction and equipment, and nonmunitions is arbitrary. Efficiency of resources put into construction and equipment may have risen less or more than efficiency of resources in the production, transportation, and distribution of consumer goods; and it may well be asked how productivity of resources in such a heterogeneous category as 'nonmunitions' can be gauged. But it seemed preferable to make the assumption, on whatever little ground could be found, then show how the customary measures have to be modified, if only to stress the questions that must be answered in any consistent estimate of national output or input in real terms.

Comparison of the indexes in Tables II 2 and 3 reveals relatively minor differences, largely because the scanty data indicate merely minor changes in the efficiency of resources embodied in the flow of goods to consumers and other components aside from munitions and war construction.

Since changes in the prices of all components are measured on the same base in Table II 3, price indexes implicit in national product can be derived (lines 4 and 5).[9] These are indexes of resource

8 See Appendix Tables II 2, 3, and 6. Actually, totals 'deflated' by final product price indexes were adjusted.

The efficiency index for the nonwar sector (see App. Table II 2, col. 3) shows only a minor decline from the latter part of 1941 to 1942; and no change from 1942 to 1943. It is quite possible that the index is biased in failing to reflect a decline in efficiency of resource use in nonwar industries in the latter part of 1942 and in 1943. Unfortunately there is no evidence upon which to estimate such a decline. If the index is indeed faulty in this respect, resource input (at 1939 prices) in the nonwar sector would be understated in 1942 and 1943.

9 This is true with the exception of governmental services to individuals (direct taxes), which are included at the same absolute level in both the current price and

TABLE II 3

Resource Price Indexes

National Product and Its Components, 1939-1943

1939 = 100

Price Indexes for Resources Embodied in	1939	1940	1941	1942	1943
1 Flow of goods to consumers (excl. gov. services)	100	104	112	128	140
2 Nonwar construction & equipment, gross	100	104	112	122	129
3 War output, gross	100	112	129	147	162
4 Gross national product	100	104	114	133	149
5 Net national product	100	104	114	136	153

All indexes are implicit: totals in current prices divided by the corresponding totals in 1939 resource prices.

prices, that is, strictly speaking, the totals to which they apply are of national resource input, not of final output.[10]

The notable features of these indexes are their rise to relatively high levels by 1943 and the acceleration of the rise after 1941. In the two years 1939-41 they rise only 14 per cent; in the following two years over 30 per cent, partly because of a fairly steep rise from 1941 to 1943 in resource prices of war output, partly because of the large increase in the weight of war output in national product.

c Conversion to final product prices

The main question here concerns the relative efficiency of resources used in munitions and war construction. The sole evidence is scattered information on changes in labor efficiency in some munitions industries (planes, merchant ships), which indicates a marked rise. There are no data that would serve even to suggest the relative efficiency of resources in munitions and war construction compared with that in similar (i.e., five 'war') industries in 1939—except again fragmentary data on loss of labor time paid for due to labor 'hoarding', difficulties of attaining a smooth flow of materials and components, and troubles arising from rapid modifications in technical specifications due to fluid conditions of active warfare.

Consequently, assumptions had to be made again. The estimates

adjusted totals. The item, however, is relatively small, and of slight effect on the implicit price indexes.

[10] Not the full total of all resource input, since resources devoted to unproductive activities (e.g., robbery or forbidden drug peddling) are presumably excluded. The total embraces only resource input in uses not explicitly recognized by society as deleterious.

arrived at by resort to them, of illustrative value, lead us to conclusions that are no more than tentative and inferential. The three
assumptions in the calculation differed in the relative efficiency
assigned to resource input for the first half of 1943. Assumption *a*
set the level of efficiency in munitions and war construction at 80;
for the other components of national product, at 105. This meant
that whatever the efficiency ratio of resources in the five 'war'
industries to resources in all 'other' industries was in 1939, the corresponding ratio in the first half of 1943 was lower by the proportion: $(105 - 80) \div 105$. Assumption *b* set the relative efficiency
level in munitions and war construction in the first half of 1943
at the efficiency *ratio* for the five 'war' industries in 1939. Assumption *c* set it higher than the corresponding ratio for the five 'war'
industries in 1939, by the proportion: $(130 - 105) \div 105$.[11]

In addition to assuming different *levels* of relative efficiency in
munitions and war construction in the first half of 1943, we assume
that they *moved* similarly between 1939 and the recent quarters,
namely: (i) that efficiency increased two-thirds from 1939 to the
first half of 1943, then another tenth in the second half of that
year; (ii) that the increase was fairly steady through 1941; (iii)
that in the last quarter of 1941, and especially in the first and second
quarters of 1942, the upward trend was damped by the precipitous
expansion of munitions and war construction; (iv) that efficiency
rose rapidly after the second quarter of 1942 as plants were completed, mass production of munitions began to hit its stride, and
the pains of rapid growth subsided; (v) that in the second half

11 The assumptions indicate nothing concerning the efficiency of resources in munitions
and war construction, on the one hand, and in all other production, on the other.
They relate directly to the ratio between two ratios: (i) the ratio in 1939 between
efficiency in the five 'war' industries and in the other sectors of national product;
(ii) the ratio between efficiency in munitions and war construction in 1943 and
efficiency in the other sectors of national product.

   Assumption *a* states that the ratio of (ii) to (i) is 0.76 (i.e., $(80 \div 105) : 1$);
assumption *b*, that it is 1.0 (i.e., $(105 \div 105) : 1$); assumption *c*, that it is 1.24
(i.e., $(130 \div 105) : 1$).

   However, the assumptions imply a relation between the efficiency of resources in
munitions and war construction in 1943 and in the five 'war' industries in 1939:
under assumption *a*, the former is at a level of 0.8 of the latter; under assumption *b*, of
1.05; under assumption *c*, of 1.3.

   The reference throughout is to the first half of 1943, the most recent period covered
in the original calculations.

of 1943 the rate of increase began to decline, reflecting the beginning of cutbacks in some of the older programs.[12]

Upon these assumptions, we convert the indexes of resource prices for munitions and war construction into indexes of final product prices, the prices being on the bases at which comparable products were valued in a prewar year like 1939 (Table II 4, line 3). Since these indexes are consistent with those for the flow of consumer goods and nonwar capital formation, indexes of price changes in national product also can be calculated (Table II 4, lines 4 and 5).

Of course, the price indexes for war output are not in terms of 1939 as 100: they would yield 100 for 1939 only if the efficiency of resource use in war production were assumed to stand in the same relation to efficiency in the other sectors of production as characterized the five 'war' industries at their 1939 productivity level. In other words, the base of the indexes is not the actual prices of war products in 1939, but what those prices would have been if the efficiency of resource use in munitions and war construction had been the same as in the five 'war' industries in 1939. The amount by which the entries in lines 3a, b, and c exceed 100 in 1939 measures the extent to which the relative efficiency of resources in war production was assumed to fall short of that in comparable industries in 1939.

If we wish to measure temporal price changes alone, i.e., not correct for any differences in the way prices measure real output in the war sector as compared with the nonwar, lines 3a, b, and c can be converted to relatives of 1939 and the results averaged (line 6). This price index rises moderately to 1942, then declines in 1943.

[12] The assumed movement in the relative efficiency of resource use, as distinct from the level assumed for the first half of 1943, is based for the years since 1941 upon a rough check with the expansion in munitions output weighted by constant prices. The three assumptions concerning the relative efficiency level in the first half of 1943 are illustrative; and the preference, in subsequent discussion, for assumption *a* is based largely upon scattered evidence of lavish (by peacetime standards) use of manpower and materials in war production.

There is no inconsistency in assuming a rapid *rise* in the relative efficiency of resource use in munitions and war construction and a low *level* compared with the efficiency in the five 'war' industries in 1939. A rapid rise could hardly be expected from levels of efficiency in 1939 that would be close to those in comparable industries which have enjoyed a long history of rising volumes and cumulative improvements in technology of operation. Yet this in itself is no proof that levels of relative efficiency of resource use in munitions and war construction by 1943 were necessarily lower than those of comparable industries in 1939.

Differences among the various price indexes in Table II 4 are as might be expected. If we allow for the lower efficiency of resource use in war production than in the comparable prewar industries, and thus for a higher price level in it, the very increase in the proportion of war output in national product causes an upward movement in the price indexes for national product as a whole. For example, under assumption *a* the over-all price index rises more than 50 per cent from 1939 to 1943 (lines 4a and 5a). The failure to allow for

TABLE II 4

Final Product Price Indexes

Three Assumptions concerning the Relative Efficiency of Resource Use in Munitions and War Construction, 1939-1943

Price Indexes for	1939	1940	1941	1942	1943
1 Flow of goods to consumers (excl. gov. services)	100	101	107	122	134
2 Nonwar construction & equipment, gross	100	101	107	116	123
3 War output, gross					
a) Assumption *a*	165	175	187	189	182
b) Assumption *b*	138	144	156	158	148
c) Assumption *c*	119	123	133	133	126
4 National income					
a) Assumption *a*	101	103	113	142	156
b) Assumption *b*	101	102	111	134	143
c) Assumption *c*	100	102	110	127	131
5 Gross national product					
a) Assumption *a*	101	103	112	139	152
b) Assumption *b*	101	102	111	132	140
c) Assumption *c*	100	102	109	125	130
6 War output, disregarding level of relative efficiency in war production	100	104	113	114	108
7 National income (based on lines 1, 2, 6)	100	101	108	120	121
8 Gross national product (based on lines 1, 2, 6)	100	101	108	119	121
9 Gross national product, Dept. of Commerce adjustment & concept	100	101	106	115	120

LINE

1 & 2 Table II 2.

3a, b, c See Appendix II.

4 & 5 Totals in current prices divided by the corresponding totals in 1939 prices (App. Tables II 11-14).

6 Arithmetic mean of relatives of lines 3a, b, and c (1939 = 100).

7 & 8 Totals in current prices (App. Table II 11) divided by the price adjusted totals (adjusted by lines 1, 2, and 6).

9 *Survey of Current Business*, April 1944, p. 6, Table 1. The concept includes in gross national product *all* government outlays.

the lower efficiency of resources in war output yields an over-all price index that rises only 19 or 20 per cent from 1939 to 1942, and in 1943 rises 1-2 per cent further (lines 7 and 8).

In its adjustment for price changes the Department of Commerce assumes that final prices of munitions do not change over time, and that they are comparable with prices in the nonwar sectors (line 9). This is tantamount to saying that a war output price index is affected solely by changes in the prices and relative weight of non-munitions, and, in the Department's calculations, also by the changes in the construction costs indexes used to 'deflate' war construction. The resulting price index is similar to an index that measures only temporal changes in the prices of war output and does not allow for the lower level of relative efficiency of resource use. Line 9 differs from line 8 only in that it is somewhat lower in 1941, 1942, and 1943, and rises slightly more from 1942 to 1943.

4 NATIONAL PRODUCT IN CONSTANT PRICES

a *The several variants*

With the alternative price indexes discussed in Section 3, national product and its components at constant price levels in several variants are computed (Table II 5). The meaning of each variant must be understood before the differences in its movement over time, in its distribution among its main components, and in the increases and declines in it and its components can be analyzed.

The variants in lines 1 are sums of resources valued at their 1939 prices. Line I 1, for example, is the sum of productive resources, weighted at their 1939 prices, i.e., at their 1939 efficiency as represented by the prices they fetched in that year, embodied in the flow of goods to consumers. A similar statement, with modifications in the description of the categories of final products into which the resources entered, can be made for lines II 1, III 1, IV 1, and V 1.

The four variants in lines 2 differ in the degree to which they allow, in the transition from the resource to the final product level of measuring munitions and war construction, for differences in the relative efficiency of resource use. Variants *a, b,* and *c* assume that resource use in munitions and war construction is at an efficiency level, relative to the rest of the economy, different from that characterizing similar types of industrial output (i.e., largely the metal working, chemical, and construction industries) in 1939. Variant *d* disregards such differences in efficiency level betwen munitions and war construction and its prewar civilian counterpart in 1939, and adjusts the value in current prices only for temporal changes in the final product prices of war goods.

The 2a lines are, then, the sums of final products weighted by their 1939 prices, on the assumption that in converting resource input in munitions and war construction into final products, the efficiency of use, relative to the rest of the economy, was in 1939 at 0.48 of the relative efficiency level of comparable peacetime industries (metal mining and manufacturing, chemicals and construc-

TABLE II 5

National Product and Resource Input, Wartime Concept, 1939-1943
1939 Final Product and Resource Prices

(billions of dollars)

	1939	1940	1941	1942	1943
I Flow of goods to consumers					
1 Resource input	64.8	66.4	69.5	66.6	67.1
2 Final product	64.8	68.0	72.7	69.8	70.3
II Nonwar capital formation, gross					
1 Resource input	13.2	16.1	18.7	7.2	2.1
2 Final product	13.2	16.5	19.6	7.6	2.2
III War output, gross					
1 Resource input	1.4	2.5	9.9	34.3	50.2
2 Final product					
a) Assumption *a*	0.8	1.6	6.9	26.5	44.6
b) Assumption *b*	1.0	1.9	8.2	31.9	54.8
c) Assumption *c*	1.1	2.3	9.6	37.8	64.8
d) Disregarding level of relative efficiency in war production	1.4	2.7	11.3	44.1	75.3
IV Net national product					
1 Resource input	72.2	77.6	90.2	99.1	109.3
2 Final product					
a) Using III 2a, net	71.6	78.7	91.3	94.9	107.0
b) Using III 2b, net	71.8	79.0	92.6	100.3	117.2
c) Using III 2c, net	71.9	79.4	94.0	106.2	127.2
d) Using III 2d, net	72.2	79.8	95.7	112.5	137.7
V Gross national product					
1 Resource input	79.4	85.0	98.1	108.1	119.4
2 Final product					
a) Using III 2a	78.8	86.1	99.2	103.9	117.1
b) Using III 2b	79.0	86.4	100.5	109.3	127.3
c) Using III 2c	79.1	86.8	101.9	115.2	137.3
d) Using III 2d	79.4	87.2	103.6	121.5	147.8

All entries from Appendix II tables.

tion) and rose to 0.88 by the last quarter of 1943. The same statement could be repeated for lines 2b and c, with changes in the ratios to 0.63 and 1.18, and 0.78 and 1.46 respectively.[13]

The 2d lines are quite different: also the sums of final products weighted by their 1939 prices, they do not allow, in the conversion of resource input in munitions and war construction into final products, for any difference in *level* of efficiency, between these industries and comparable peacetime industries, relative to the rest of the economy. They do reflect, however, the large upward *movement* in the efficiency of resource use in munitions and war construction.

The distinction between the estimates at resource and at final product levels is clear; and which is chosen depends primarily on the uses to which they are to be put. Similarly, the choice between the final product totals that do (a, b, c) and do not (d) allow for differences in levels of relative efficiency between war and peacetime production of comparable character is also clear; for any purposes in which national product, in real terms, for prewar and war years is to be compared and in which the proportion of war and other output is to be established in final product terms, variants of the *a-c* type alone are suitable.

But the choice among the three variants based on different assumptions concerning the relative efficiency of resources in munitions and war production is not easy; for it is determined by differences in the validity of assumptions concerning a phenomenon extremely difficult to observe at all accurately—not by theoretical criteria. As already indicated, preference for one of these three variants (or any of this type using different levels of relative efficiency of war production) cannot be grounded upon much tangible evidence and is largely a matter of judgment.

As far as national product and its distribution by final product categories are concerned, the choice among variants *a, b,* and *c* (and perhaps any others of similar character that may reasonably be devised) is of quantitative importance for 1942 and 1943 alone. Before 1942 war output, no matter how measured, was too small a proportion of national product for differences in its price adjustment to have much effect. Even in 1942 the spread among national product totals in the three variants is only somewhat over 10 per

13 Under the assumptions concerning both relative levels and movement discussed in Section 3c.

cent. Not until 1943 do the quantitative effects of the choice among the three variants become decisive.

We definitely prefer variant *a,* with its assumption that resource use in war production in the first half of 1943 was still below comparable prewar industries in relative efficiency. The efficiency we are concerned with is that in munitions and war construction in 1943 as compared with similar peacetime industries of 1939, not as compared with it in munitions and war construction in 1942, 1941, or 1939, or that of resources in 'other' industries in 1943 or any earlier year. The judgment is solely that the efficiency of resources in munitions and war construction in the first half of 1943 was some 20 per cent lower than that of resource use in comparable prewar industries in 1939. In other words, utilization of labor (measured, e.g., by idle hours out of the total paid for or by diversion to less essential jobs to fill gaps); of materials (measured, e.g., by rates of consumption compared with those at more mature stages of technology); of machinery (measured at input rates per unit, not at time rates, compared again with the practices of the older and gradually developing industries of peacetime) was, in the first half of 1943, still below the prewar par.

This statement should not be interpreted as an adverse verdict upon this country's enterprise or as depreciation of its enormous accomplishment after it entered the war. On the contrary, to be able to assume that relative efficiency in war production was no more than one-fifth less than that of comparable peacetime industries is a matter for congratulation when we think of the pressure to turn out munitions in huge quantities, the rapidly changing demands of warfare, and the drains upon manpower and management by calls into the military services. But just as it would be unfair to minimize the gigantic productive task met, so would it be misleading to ignore the patent fact that resources were not used as economically as they might have been had the more efficient methods feasible with slower growth under more normal competitive conditions been possible. Regardless of the validity of the specific figure used in assumption *a* (which should perhaps be somewhat larger or smaller), we believe that assigning to war production a *lower* level of relative efficiency in the first half of 1943 than existed in similar industries before the war is decidedly more justifiable than putting it on the same or a higher level.

b *Increase, 1939-1943*

We discuss only the two estimates that seem preferable: resource input or national product at final product prices under assumption *a*.

National product, both gross and net, is roughly 50 per cent greater in 1943 than in 1939 (Table II 6, col. 6). Of this increase, somewhat more than half occurred before this country entered the war (col. 1 and 5). The percentage increase in national product during the two years of participation is somewhat less than that during the two years of neutrality.

The increases in the Department of Commerce totals and in such

TABLE II 6

National Product and Resource Input, Wartime Concept
Percentage Increase, Selected Periods
1939 Prices, Several Variants

	1939-1941	1941-1942	1939-1942	1942-1943	1941-1943	1939-1943
	(1)	(2)	(3)	(4)	(5)	(6)
I Net national product						
1 Resource input	24.9	9.9	37.3	10.3	21.2	51.4
2 Final product						
a) Regarding relative efficiency in war production, assumption *a**	27.5	3.9	32.5	12.8	17.2	49.4
d) Disregarding level of relative efficiency in war production	32.5	17.6	55.8	22.4	43.9	90.7
II Gross national product						
1 Resource input	23.6	10.2	36.1	10.5	21.7	50.4
2 Final product						
a) Regarding relative efficiency in war production, assumption *a**	25.9	4.7	31.9	12.7	18.0	48.6
d) Disregarding level of relative efficiency in war production	30.5	17.3	53.0	21.6	42.7	86.1
III Other measures						
1 Dept. of Commerce G.N.P., 1939 prices						
a) Dept. of Commerce concept	26.7	18.1	49.7	17.1	38.3	75.3
b) Adj. to our concept	31.7	20.1	58.2	18.3	42.1	87.2
2 FRB industrial production index	48.6	22.8	82.6	20.1	47.5	119.3
***Net national product**						
b) Assumption *b*	29.0	8.3	39.7	16.8	26.6	63.2
c) Assumption *c*	30.7	13.0	47.7	19.8	35.3	76.9
Gross national product						
b) Assumption *b*	27.2	8.8	38.4	16.5	26.7	61.1
c) Assumption *c*	28.8	13.1	45.6	19.2	34.7	73.6

Entries under I and II based on Table II 5. Entries under III based on Department of Commerce figures and the Federal Reserve Board index (revised as of Oct. 1943).

widely used measures of industrial output as the Federal Reserve Board index are larger. Gross national product, based upon the Department of Commerce concept and price adjustment, rises 75 per cent; and the percentage rise from 1941 to 1943 is much greater than from 1939 to 1941. Readjusted to our concept (to exclude prewar business taxes), it rises 87 per cent from 1939 to 1943; and again the percentage rise after 1941 is much greater than during the preceding two years. The Federal Reserve Board index, which would naturally rise more since it is more heavily weighted by industrial commodity production, rises 119 per cent from 1939 to 1943; the percentage rise from 1941 to 1943 is about the same as from 1939 to 1941. The difference between our estimates and those of the Department of Commerce is due largely to a different treatment of the value of war output; that between our estimates and the Federal Reserve Board index is due partly to a difference in coverage and partly to a different treatment of the productivity of factors in the war industries.[14]

The rates of increase in our national product totals at resource or at final product prices are in themselves not unusual. In the two decades for which annual estimates are available, 1919-38, there are increases of relatively the same size. From 1921 to 1923 net national product in 1929 prices rose 25 per cent and gross national product (wartime concept) 22 per cent; from 1935 to 1937, 24 and 22 per cent. These increases compare with a 25-27 per cent increase from 1939 to 1941; and with an increase of either 17 or 22 per cent from 1941 to 1943. From 1933 to 1937 net national product in constant prices increased 49 per cent and gross national product 43 per cent, which compares with roughly 50 per cent from 1939 to 1943. From 1933 to 1936 the former increased 38 per cent, the latter 33 per cent, compared with 33 and 32 per cent from 1939 to 1942.[15]

14 The FRB index is based, for recent years, upon man hour input in many war industries, weighted by productivity levels extrapolated from 1939. No allowance is made for possibly lower efficiency levels in the war industries relatively to those of comparable industries in 1939.

15 All figures for national income and for gross national product 1919-38 are from estimates recently revised for *National Product since 1869*. The comparison should properly be confined to the variant at final product prices, since the national income figures have been adjusted for price changes with the help of final product price indexes. But during relatively short periods in the more 'normal' peace years, the

These numerical comparisons disregard the phase of the business cycle the initial years represent. Each period selected from the two decades 1919-38 begins with a year of deep depression, either 1921 or 1933, with the sole exception of 1935-37, and even by 1935 cyclical expansion had fallen short of the preceding cyclical peak in total output (as measured by national income in constant prices). Under such conditions national product in real terms may easily rise by substantial percentages within a fairly short period. In contrast, 1939 was not a year of depression: the level of activity, again as measured by national income or gross national product in constant prices, was much higher than in the preceding peak year in the business cycle, 1937. This consideration, together with the probable continuation of the rise that began in 1938 through 1944, and the bias of the comparison against the present period because of the more careful adjustment for price differentials and changes that tend to overvalue product in *any* expansion, leads to the conclusion that the present period of sustained and marked rise in the real value of national product, which has already lasted six years, is an achievement unique in our economy in recent decades.

However, other factors must be taken into account. First, even though 1939 was a year of more than full recovery from the cyclical depression of 1938, the levels of national product in constant prices do not compare favorably with 1929; and as indicated more fully in Part III, there are many evidences that more resources could have been put to use. A substantial part of the subsequent rise was facilitated by this slack, which greatly exceeded that in the 1920's. Second, even disregarding the whole question of the ultimate net

difference in movement between resource input and final product levels would not be sizable.

It may be argued that the comparison is improper, since in any cyclical expansion the proportion of national product accounted for by the less efficient 'new' industries (similar to munitions and war construction) may increase; and a procedure like that used here to put final products on a comparable valuation basis would tend to accelerate the rise of the price indexes, thereby retarding the rise in the price adjusted totals. No such price adjustment was applied to the estimates for 1919-38.

The validity of this argument depends upon the correctness of the assumption that there is a substantial rise during cyclical expansions in the proportion of national product accounted for by the less efficient 'new' industries (beyond the rising secular trend in their share). It is to be doubted that such an increase even approximates the degree to which the share of war output increased in 1942 and 1943, at least for areas in peacetime economy so 'new' and so far below comparable industries in relative efficiency as were munitions and war construction.

contribution of war output to future social welfare, between 1939 and 1944, as in any cyclical expansion, resources shifted from the nonmarket to the market area; such a shift, as always, meant a reduction in the flow from the nonmarket area of goods of a type rarely taken account of in measuring national product. Yet the reduction in the supply of these nonmarket goods (largely services of housewives and other members of the family) must have been much greater during this recent period than during the prewar cyclical expansions; and the offsets to the rise in the volume of goods turned out by the market sector must have been all the greater. Perhaps as our data improve, further research will succeed in measuring the nonmarket sectors of the economy (in addition to such few items as are now covered, e.g., products retained by farmers and imputed rent); and thus lead to a more comprehensive measure of the total flow of final product. This more comprehensive measure would undoubtedly show a smaller relative rise from 1939 to 1943 than the present estimates.[16]

c *Share of war output*

The changing ratio of war output to national product is of particular interest in wartime as an indicator of the proportion of resources or final products devoted to war. As a measure of the full impact of the war upon the national economy, it has serious limitations: it disregards the effect of the war upon the capital structure of the country, while its meaning in terms of effects upon the welfare of the inhabitants is obviously contingent upon the level of national product per capita, the rate at which civilian supply per capita declines, and the distribution of consumer goods. However, it is a rough approximation to what is wanted; and in view of its

[16] The analysis of the estimates we present could, perhaps, have been made more pointed had we attempted to measure the rise in national product in relation to the underlying long term trend instead of from a given year. However, the establishment of such a trend is beset with difficulties; and its values at the end of the long period to which the trend line would have to be fitted would be subject to especially wide margins of error.

Another refinement of the estimates in Table II 6 (and in Tables II 7 and 8) is to base them on quarterly rather than annual totals. These quarterly estimates, presented in Appendix II, can be used in calculations that span the full period and distinguish between the quarters before and after Pearl Harbor. Since they are approximate and their margin of error wider, it did not seem necessary to go beyond the annual totals.

wide current usage, its movement is established on the basis of our estimates.

The share of war output increased rapidly from 1939 to the first half of 1943—from 1 or 2 per cent to a percentage ranging from 38 to 45; also, as would be expected, most sharply from 1941 to 1942 (Table II 7). The Department of Commerce estimates are similar. Only when we apply its method of price adjustment to our concept does the share in 1942 and 1943 greatly exceed that measured here at the resource level. The difference is not more, partly because our adjustment corrects the prices of both consumer goods and war output for upward biases.

The difference between the share of war output for 1942 in final product prices (variant *a*) and the Department's is greater. Indeed, the outstanding feature of Table II 7 is the difference for all years

TABLE II 7

War Output as a Percentage of National Product, Wartime Concept, 1939-1943

1939 Prices, Several Variants

	1939	1940	1941	1942	1943
I Net national product					
1 Resource input	1.9	3.2	10.6	33.8	44.5
2 Final product					
a) Regarding relative efficiency in war production, assumption *a**	1.1	2.0	7.2	27.1	40.2
d) Disregarding level of relative efficiency in war production	1.9	3.4	11.5	38.5	53.5
II Gross national product					
1 Resource input	1.8	2.9	10.1	31.7	42.0
2 Final product					
a) Regarding relative efficiency in war production, assumption *a**	1.0	1.9	7.0	25.5	38.1
d) Disregarding level of relative efficiency in war production	1.8	3.1	10.9	36.3	50.9
III Other measures					
1 Dept. of Commerce G.N.P., 1939 prices					
a) Dept. of Commerce concept	1.6	2.8	10.9	34.8	46.7
b) Adj. to our concept	1.8	3.1	11.7	36.7	48.8
*Net national product					
b) Assumption *b*	1.4	2.4	8.5	31.0	45.4
c) Assumption *c*	1.5	2.9	9.9	34.8	49.7
Gross national product					
b) Assumption *b*	1.3	2.2	8.2	29.2	43.0
c) Assumption *c*	1.4	2.6	9.4	32.8	47.2

See source notes to Table II 6.

between the shares at the resource and final product levels (lines 1 and 2a). In terms of resource input, war output accounts for a larger share of the national total than when it is adjusted for the relative efficiency of resource use and expressed in terms of final product. This difference is natural since we assume that, owing to a lower efficiency of resource use in war production, the quantity of final war products turned out was less than that resulting in peacetime from the same input of resources in comparable industries. The difference had narrowed materially by 1943, and if efficiency continues to improve, may vanish, or perhaps even change sign.

d Source of increase in war output
The output of commodities and services for the armed conflict can be augmented by shifting resources from civilian to war production, by increasing the total resources put into active use, and by both methods. Comparison of the increase in war output with the changes in the nonwar components of national product and in national product itself in current prices indicates the financial sources of war output, but not the resource or final product balance. To show how misleading totals in current prices can be as measures of resources or final products in periods of rapid differential price shifts, they, together with the totals and components in constant resource or product prices are given in Table II 8.

From 1939 to 1941 the several variants of national product and its components in constant prices are roughly similar (Table II 8, Part A). There is a substantial increase in national product and in each of its three chief components—war output, flow of consumer goods, and nonwar capital formation (private gross capital formation plus nonwar government outlay in the Department of Commerce total). The increase in war output is a fraction of the total increase in national product—in all variants less than a half, and ranging in general from one-fourth to somewhat over two-fifths. Even the totals in current prices are fairly similar, largely because prices rose little.

The picture from 1941 to 1943 is quite different (Table II 8, Part B). In general, war output climbs precipitously—in every variant appreciably more than national product. The other components decline markedly, particularly nonwar capital formation (and, in the Department of Commerce concept, nonwar expenditures

TABLE II 8

National Product and Its Components, Wartime Concept, Changes, 1939-1941 and 1941-1943, 1939 Prices, Several Variants
(billions of dollars)

	PART A 1939 TO 1941				PART B 1941 TO 1943			
	War output (1)	Flow of goods to consumers (2)	Other components (3)	National product (4)	War output (5)	Flow of goods to consumers (6)	Other components (7)	National product (8)
I Net national product								
1 Resource input	8.2	4.7	5.1	18.0	39.0	−2.4	−17.5	19.1
2 Final product								
a) Regarding relative efficiency in war production, assumption a*	5.8	7.9	6.0	19.7	36.4	−2.4	−18.3	15.7
d) Disregarding level of relative efficiency in war production	9.6	7.9	6.0	23.5	62.7	−2.4	−18.3	42.0
II Gross national product								
1 Resource input	8.5	4.7	5.5	18.7	40.3	−2.4	−16.6	21.3
2 Final product								
a) Regarding relative efficiency in war production, assumption a*	6.1	7.9	6.4	20.4	37.7	−2.4	−17.4	17.9
d) Disregarding level of relative efficiency in war production	9.9	7.9	6.4	24.2	64.0	−2.4	−17.4	44.2
III Other measures								
1 Dept. of Commerce G.N.P. in 1939 prices								
a) Dept. of Commerce concept	10.8	8.0	4.9	23.7	60.3	1.1	−18.4	43.0
b) Adj. to our concept	10.8	8.0	6.4	25.2	60.3	1.1	−17.4	44.0
IV National product, current prices								
1 Net	11.1	12.9	7.0	31.0	67.0	16.4	−19.5	63.9
2 Gross	11.4	12.9	7.7	32.0	68.5	16.4	−18.2	66.7
***Net national product**								
b) Assumption b	6.9	7.9	6.0	20.8	45.3	−2.4	−18.3	24.6
c) Assumption c	8.2	7.9	6.0	22.1	53.9	−2.4	−18.3	33.2
Gross national product								
b) Assumption b	7.2	7.9	6.4	21.5	46.6	−2.4	−17.4	26.8
c) Assumption c	8.5	7.9	6.4	22.8	55.2	−2.4	−17.4	35.4

See notes to Tables II 5, 6, and 7. Entries under IV from Table II 1.

of government, although the decline in it is minor). But the several variants differ in the degree to which the increase in war output in each is associated with the increase in national product or with the declines in the nonwar components. Estimates based on our concept, at both resource and final product levels (variant *a*), indicate that one-half (or somewhat less) is due to the increase in national product, the other half to the decline in nonwar capital formation and the very minor drop in the flow of consumer goods.

In the Department of Commerce estimates, whether based upon its own concept or adjusted to our concept, the increase in national product amounts to over 70 per cent of the increase in war output. The decline in the other components, i.e., chiefly in private gross capital formation, amounts to less than one-third of the increase in war output; the rest is accounted for by a minor rise in the flow of consumer goods.[17]

The picture is even more strikingly different when we assume that the increase in war output is associated with the increase in national product in current prices. In this case, well over 90 per cent of the increase in war output is accounted for by the increase in national product, and only 3 to 5 per cent by the net reduction in the nonwar components combined. Obviously the impression that the tremendous increase in war output has been attained to such a preponderant extent by an increase in national product and to such a minor extent by drafts upon nonwar output—an impression that can all too easily be formed on the basis of current prices—is far from the truth, if the analysis of national product in real terms, as suggested by the upper part of Table II 8, is at all valid.

5 SUMMARY

a) Changes in prices over time and differentials in pricing bases between the nonwar and war sectors are large during a major war. Consequently, estimates of national product and its components in current prices are misleading as indexes of movements in it and in the shares of its components in 'real' terms, i.e., as physical vol-

[17] In this calculation the full increase in national product is counted as a source of the increase in war output. The results would be practically the same were we to subtract the increase in the flow of consumer goods from the increase in national product, and treat the remainder alone as a source of augmented war output.

umes weighted by prices constant over time and consistent as to base.

b) In translating totals in current into totals in constant prices, both changes in prices over time and the differences in pricing bases between war and nonwar output must be taken into account. Only thus can a continued series of comparable estimates, spanning both prewar and war years, be made.

c) Such an adjustment is attempted here on two levels. First, indexes, based on 1939, of resource prices were computed for 1939 to 1943. Their application to totals in current prices yielded estimates of *resource input,* total and for the main components of final product; resources being weighted at 1939 prices, i.e., at their 1939 relative efficiency levels. Second, with the help of assumptions concerning the relative efficiency of resource use in munitions and war construction, all indexes were converted into measures of changes in the prices of final products. Their application to totals in current prices yielded estimates of *final product,* total and for the main components, weighted by their 1939 prices (war goods priced on a base comparable with that of peace type products).

d) National product adjusted for changes in the prices of resources (i.e., input of resources at their 1939 efficiency and price levels) increased about 50 per cent from 1939 to 1943. In terms of final product and on the most plausible assumption concerning the relative efficiency of resource use in munitions and war construction, it increased somewhat less. Both increases are appreciably less than those in the Department of Commerce gross national product totals in 1939 prices. Estimates based on the Department's concept and price adjustments increase 75 per cent; those based on our concept but using the Department's price adjustments, 87 per cent.

e) An increase in either gross or net national product, in constant prices, of about 50 per cent during four years can be matched in peacetime (e.g., from 1933 to 1937). The recent increase is unusual in that it came not after a deep cyclical trough but after 1939, which cannot be described as a year of depression, for its levels of over-all output were above those of the immediately preceding cyclical peak (1937).

f) Both the resource input and the preferred final product estimates increase from 1941 to 1943 somewhat less than from 1939 to 1941. In contrast, the Department of Commerce estimates of gross national product in constant prices increase from 1941 to 1943 almost one and a half times more than from 1939 to 1941.

g) In both total resource input and final product, the share of the war sector rises precipitously—from 1 or 2 per cent in 1939 to about 40 in 1943; the share of the nonwar sectors declines correspondingly in 1943. Our ratios of war output to national product at the final output level are lower (38) than those based on Department of Commerce gross national product totals in 1939 prices (47). In terms of resource input, the share of the war sector in our estimates (42 per cent) differs less from that in the Department of Commerce's.

h) From 1939 to 1941 the increase in the volume of resources devoted to war production or in the final products represented by it was merely a fraction (roughly one-third to four-tenths) of the increase in total resource input or final output. Resource input or final output represented by the flow of consumer goods and nonwar capital formation also increased substantially. Totals in current prices and the Department of Commerce gross national product in constant prices all show these relations.

i) From 1941 to 1943, in contrast, the increase in the volume of resources devoted to war production or in the final products represented by it was much greater than in total resource input or final output. Our estimates of the national totals of either resource input or final product rose one-half (or somewhat less) as much as war output; the compensating changes are a marked decline in nonwar capital formation and a minor drop in the flow of consumer goods. Hence at least one-half of the increase in war output was associated with drafts upon nonwar capital formation and (to a minor extent) upon the flow of consumer goods.

j) The Department of Commerce totals in constant prices show a different picture. From 1941 to 1943 the rise in national product in constant prices accounts for over seven-tenths of the increase in war output; i.e., less than three-tenths of the increase is accounted for by a decrease in the nonwar sectors, largely nonwar capital formation. In other words, our estimates, which tend to 'deflate' war output to terms comparable with nonwar, indicate for 1941-43 a greater dependence of the increase in the war sector upon contraction in the nonwar sectors, and relatively less upon the increase in national product.

Calculation of Quarterly Estimates in 1939 Prices
1 FLOW OF GOODS TO CONSUMERS

a *Final products*

The basic data are those of the Department of Commerce on consumers' outlay. To the annual estimates of consumers' outlay in 1939 prices the prewar total of direct taxes, $3.1 billion, is added.

The Department of Commerce adjustment for price changes consists largely in reweighting the BLS prices of consumers' commodities and services. We attempted to improve the adjustment by comparing the 'deflated' totals for food and clothing prepared by the Department of Commerce with measures of the physical volume of commodity flow.[18]

For about 75 food items, representing more than 95 per cent by value of all foods purchased by civilians, the Food Distribution Administration has estimated the amount flowing into civilian channels, i.e., after allowance for military takings and net exports. These items were weighted by consumers' expenditures in 1941. Since no data are available for 1939 we could not check for an upward bias in consumers' expenditures from 1939 to 1941. The weighted FDA estimates were therefore linked to the estimate of deflated expenditures for 1941, giving estimates of expenditures in constant prices 4 and 6 per cent lower than those of the Department of Commerce for 1942 and 1943, respectively.

It is unlikely that inventory changes can account for any considerable part of these differences. The FDA consumption estimates allow for inventory changes at the early stages of the distribution process, and the rather sketchy data on retail inventories do not indicate much liquidation in either 1942 or 1943. Nor could a higher degree of fabrication account for an accelerated upward movement in consumers' expenditures. Military and lend-lease takings, heavily weighted with highly processed items, are sufficient to explain the slightly greater employment in the processing industries in 1942 and 1943.

The price adjusted totals for clothing could be checked with the help of the Federal Reserve Board index of the output of clothing and shoes for civilians; raw materials allocated to civilian output;

[18] For the basis of the Department's price adjustment, see 'Price Deflators for Consumer Commodities and Capital Equipment, 1929-42', by Henry Shavell, *Survey of Current Business,* May 1943, pp. 13-21; also Part II, note 6.

military takings; and man hours of employment in apparel industries. The consensus of these data indicates an overstatement of
expenditures, when adjusted by current price indexes for clothing
and shoes, of roughly 15 per cent in 1942 and 26 per cent in 1943,
even after adjustment for discrepancies that might be attributed to
a reduction in inventories.[19]

Both adjustments reflect probably not only a rise in prices but
also quality uptrading of a kind that occurs when incomes rise; and
the disparity between the Department of Commerce 'deflated' totals
and the physical volume we used may be due also to a possible over-
valuation of retail sales in the Department's estimates of the flow
of civilian foods and clothing in current prices. For these reasons
it cannot be claimed that for these two specific categories the implicit price indexes constructed above measure the price rise more
accurately than the indexes used by the Department of Commerce
in calculating the 'deflated' totals.

But even if the adjustments overstate the rise in the prices of
food and clothing, we thought it best to include them fully. For
no other commodity and service group is account taken of the failure of currently available price indexes to reflect completely quality
deterioration, forced uptrading, and shifts of consumers to higher
priced localities. Any overadjustment for food and clothing would
probably be more than offset by the failure to adjust the 'deflated'
totals in all other categories of consumer goods (App. Table II 1).

From the annual indexes of final product prices of consumer
goods we estimated consumers' outlay in 1939 prices annually. To
get the total flow of goods to individuals and households we added
$3.1 billion per year to allow for the value of direct governmental
services to individuals. The quarterly totals for 1939-41 are Department of Commerce estimates. Those for 1942 and 1943 are
interpolations within our annual totals in 1939 prices (App. Table
II 1) on the basis of the quarterly totals in 1939 prices as estimated
by the Department of Commerce (App. Table II 2, col. 1 and 2).

b *Resource input*
For reasons discussed in the text, we need estimates of the flow of
consumer goods not only in 1939 final product prices but also in

---

[19] Because of the confidential classification of the underlying data, the detailed calculations cannot be shown here.

terms of resource input at 1939 prices of resources. The simplest way to get this series is to construct an index of the efficiency of resource use in the production and distribution of consumer goods; then apply an adjustment based upon this efficiency index directly to the value of consumer goods in 1939 final product prices.

Except for scattered data on changes in physical output per man hour for a few manufacturing and mining industries and utilities (published chiefly by the Bureau of Labor Statistics, Productivity and Technological Development Division), there is no information on changes in the efficiency of resources used in the production of consumer goods or in other nonwar categories. The few data suggest that the annual gain in productivity since 1939 has been moderate, not more than 2 or 3 per cent; that it virtually ceased by 1942; and that in recent quarters, as the scale of operations in many

APPENDIX TABLE II 1

Flow of Goods to Consumers, 1939 Prices
Revised Estimates Compared with Department of Commerce Estimates
(dollar figures in billions; base year for indexes, 1939)

	1942	1943
A COMMODITIES		
I Department of Commerce		
1 Total, current prices	54.4	61.7
2 Total, 1939 prices	43.4	45.4
3 Implicit price index $(1 \div 2)100$	125.3	135.9
II Our Estimates		
4 Total, 1939 prices	41.2	41.8
5 Implicit price index $(1 \div 4)100$	132.0	147.6
B SERVICES		
1 Total, current prices	27.6	29.2
2 Total, 1939 prices	25.4	25.4
3 Implicit price index	108.7	115.0
C TOTAL (excl. direct government services to individuals)		
I Department of Commerce		
1 Total, current prices	82.0	91.0
2 Total, 1939 prices	68.8	70.8
3 Implicit price index	119.2	128.5
II Our Estimates		
4 Total, 1939 prices	66.6	67.2
5 Implicit price index	123.1	135.4

Department of Commerce estimates in current and 1939 prices from *Survey of Current Business,* April 1944, p. 8, Table 3, and p. 13, Table 10. Because of rounding, details will not necessarily check.

Flow of Goods to Consumers, Current and 1939 Prices, Quarterly, 1939-1943
(dollar figures in billions, seasonally adjusted annual rates)

YEAR & QUARTER	TOTAL Current prices	TOTAL 1939 final product prices	EFFICIENCY INDEX	ADJ. IN (2)	RESOURCE INPUT 1939 prices
	(1)	(2)	(3)	(4)	(5)
1939	64.8	64.8	100.0	0.0	64.8
I	63.5	63.7	99.1	0.6	64.3
II	64.1	64.5	99.7	0.2	64.7
III	65.1	64.8	100.3	—0.2	64.6
IV	66.3	65.9	100.9	—0.6	65.3
1940	68.8	68.0	102.5	—1.6	66.4
I	67.7	67.1	101.5	—0.9	66.2
II	68.1	67.4	102.2	—1.4	66.0
III	69.0	68.2	102.8	—1.8	66.4
IV	70.3	69.3	103.4	—2.2	67.1
1941	77.7	72.7	104.8	—3.2	69.5
I	74.1	72.2	104.0	—2.7	69.5
II	76.8	73.0	104.6	—3.1	69.9
III	80.4	74.3	105.1	—3.5	70.8
IV	79.5	71.4	105.5	—3.6	67.8
1942	85.1	69.8	105.1	—3.2	66.6
I	83.4	71.1	105.3	—3.4	67.7
II	82.6	68.3	105.1	—3.2	65.1
III	85.9	69.7	105.0	—3.2	66.5
IV	88.5	70.1	105.0	—3.2	66.9
1943	94.1	70.3	105.0	—3.2	67.1
I	93.4	70.6	105.0	—3.2	67.4
II	92.5	69.1	105.0	—3.1	66.0
III	94.2	70.6	105.0	—3.2	67.4
IV	96.1	71.2	105.0	—3.2	68.0

COLUMN

1 Sum of consumer goods and services (*Survey of Current Business,* April 1944, p. 12, Table 7, line 14, and p. 13, Table 10, line 16) and an allowance for direct personal taxes of $3.1 billion per year—an average of direct personal taxes for 1936-38 (*ibid.,* May 1942, p. 12, Table 4, line 10).

2 Sum of estimates for (a) nondurable commodities; (b) durable commodities; (c) services, excluding direct government services to individuals; (d) direct government services. (a) for 1939-41 is from the Department of Commerce; for 1942 and 1943 annual totals of the Department of Commerce, modified by the adjustments for food and clothing categories as described in the text and interpolated by quarters on the basis of Department of Commerce quarterly estimates in 1939 prices. (b) and (c) are from the Department of Commerce. (d) is assumed to be $3.1 billion per year throughout the period.

3 Assumed, see text.

4 100(col. 2, excl. direct government services, divided by col. 3) — (col. 2, excl. direct government services).

5 Col. 2 *plus* adjustments in col. 4.

Because of rounding, details will not necessarily check.

civilian industries shrank and dilution of labor and other resources took place, efficiency per resource unit may have diminished.

The efficiency index in Appendix Table II 2, column 3, an unwarrantedly precise quantitative summary, is intended to be illustrative rather than substantive. It rises mildly to 1942, then remains stable through most of 1942 and all 1943. The adjustment it necessitates is calculated for the flow of goods to consumers, excluding direct governmental services (col. 4). The application of this adjustment to the total flow of goods to consumers in 1939 final product prices (col. 2) yields an estimate of the resource input equivalent of this flow in 1939 resource prices (col. 5). Because the changes during the period in the efficiency index are so minor, resource input and final product output move in substantially the same way, except for the somewhat more moderate rise from 1939 to 1943 in the former.

2 NONWAR CAPITAL FORMATION

The quarterly and annual totals of nonwar gross capital formation in current prices (App. Table II 3, col. 1) are the sum of corresponding totals of private gross capital formation as estimated by the Department of Commerce, and public nonwar construction—the sum of appropriate categories of public construction in the detailed estimates of the Department. The totals net of depreciation and depletion (col. 2) are the difference between column 1 and the estimated consumption of nonwar durable capital. The latter is in turn the sum of depreciation and depletion on private durable capital, as estimated by the Department of Commerce, and of an allowance for the depreciation on public construction, set roughly at $1 billion per year throughout the period.

For an adjustment of nonwar capital formation to 1939 final product prices (col. 3 and 4) we rely again on Department of Commerce estimates. The main component of column 3, private gross capital formation, in 1939 final product prices, is a Department estimate. In this price adjustment the Department uses indexes of construction costs, prices of capital equipment goods, prices of commodities (in connection with inventory changes), and so on. The methods are briefly described in the *Survey of Current Business,* March 1943 (notes to Table 1, pp. 19-20). For the other component of column 3, public nonwar construction, the values in current prices are adjusted for price changes by the Department of Commerce index for its construction component of private gross capital formation.

To pass from nonwar gross capital formation in 1939 final product prices to net, we subtract from the former depreciation and depletion valued at 1939 prices. To obtain this subtrahend, depreciation and depletion in current prices was adjusted for price changes by an index compiled from Department of Commerce data on the construction and durable equipment components of private gross capital formation. Since current price changes are presumably damped in the total values of capital goods subject to depreciation

APPENDIX TABLE II 3

Nonwar Capital Formation, Current and 1939 Prices

Quarterly, 1939-1943

(billions of dollars, seasonally adjusted annual rates)

	TOTALS					RESOURCE INPUT	
YEAR & QUARTER	CURRENT PRICES		1939 FINAL PRODUCT PRICES		ADJ. FOR TRANSITION TO RESOURCE PRICES	1939 RESOURCE PRICES	
	Gross	Net	Gross	Net		Gross	Net
	(1)	(2)	(3)	(4)	(5)	(6)	(7)
1939	13.2	6.0	13.2	6.0	0.0	13.2	6.0
I	12.7	5.5	12.6	5.4	0.1	12.7	5.5
II	11.6	4.4	11.6	4.4	0.0	11.6	4.4
III	12.5	5.3	12.5	5.3	0.0	12.5	5.3
IV	16.1	8.8	16.1	8.8	—0.1	16.0	8.7
1940	16.7	9.3	16.5	9.1	—0.4	16.1	8.7
I	16.6	9.3	16.4	9.1	—0.2	16.2	8.9
II	14.8	7.4	14.7	7.3	—0.3	14.4	7.0
III	16.5	9.1	16.4	9.0	—0.4	16.0	8.6
IV	18.8	11.3	18.5	11.1	—0.6	17.9	10.5
1941	20.9	13.0	19.6	12.0	—0.9	18.7	11.1
I	19.3	11.7	18.6	11.1	—0.7	17.9	10.4
II	20.8	13.0	19.8	12.2	—0.9	18.9	11.3
III	21.4	13.4	19.9	12.2	—1.0	18.9	11.2
IV	22.2	14.0	20.0	12.2	—1.0	19.0	11.2
1942	8.8	0.1	7.6	—0.6	—0.4	7.2	—1.0
I	14.7	6.2	12.8	4.8	—0.6	12.2	4.2
II	11.8	3.1	10.1	1.9	—0.5	9.6	1.4
III	5.5	—3.4	4.8	—3.5	—0.2	4.6	—3.7
IV	3.1	—5.9	2.7	—5.7	—0.1	2.6	—5.8
1943	2.7	—6.5	2.2	—6.3	—0.1	2.1	—6.4
I	2.7	—6.3	2.2	—6.3	—0.1	2.1	—6.4
II	1.9	—7.1	1.6	—6.9	—0.1	1.5	—7.0
III	3.4	—5.6	2.6	—5.9	—0.1	2.5	—6.0
IV	3.0	—6.0	2.2	—6.3	—0.1	2.1	—6.4

Notes to Appendix Table II 3

COLUMN

1 Sum of private gross capital formation (*Survey of Current Business,* April 1944, p. 12, Table 7, line 8, and p. 13, Table 10, line 8) and public nonwar construction, defined as public excluding residential, military and naval, and nonresidential industrial (for 1939-42: *ibid.,* May 1943, p. 10, Table 7; for 1943, by addition of monthly entries: *ibid.,* April 1944, p. S-4).

2 Col. 1 minus depreciation on both private capital (*ibid.,* April 1944, p. 14, Table 13, line 3, with minor changes to allow for a more gradual quarterly movement) and public nonwar construction (roughly estimated to be $1 billion per year throughout the period).

3 Sum of private gross capital formation in 1939 prices (Department of Commerce) and public nonwar construction (estimates in current prices, from col. 1, adjusted for price changes by the Department of Commerce index for its construction component of private gross capital formation).

4 Col. 3 minus depreciation and depletion, adjusted to 1939 prices by a price index derived from the Department of Commerce quarterly data for the construction and durable equipment components of private gross capital formation (in current and 1939 prices). One-half of the rise in the current prices of construction and equipment was allowed in the index used to adjust the depreciation and depletion allowance for price changes.

5 Based on the assumed efficiency index in App. Table II 2, col. 3. The adjustment is equal to 100(col. 3 ÷ efficiency index) — col. 3.

6 Col. 3 *plus* adjustments in col. 5.

7 Col. 4 *plus* adjustments in col. 5.

Because of rounding, details will not necessarily check.

and depletion, only one-half of the rise in the current prices of construction and equipment was included in the index. This procedure is crude. But in view of the difficulties of a proper translation of depreciation to a reproduction value base, the small annual change, and the smallness of the item relative to total national product, it did not seem worth while to attempt more laborious calculations.

Nonwar capital formation in 1939 final product prices is adjusted to resource input levels by the same efficiency index as consumer goods in Appendix Table II 2. Lack of specific data is the reason for this rather arbitrary procedure. The adjustment (App. Table II 3, col. 5) is then applied to gross capital formation in 1939 final product prices (col. 3) to yield column 6. Net nonwar capital formation in 1939 resource prices (col. 7) is the difference between gross (col. 6) and the depreciation and depletion in 1939 prices used to pass from column 3 to 4.

3 War Output

a *Resource input*

For reasons indicated in the text, the first approach to the adjustment of war output for price changes must be through the prices of resources. Consequently, we must reverse the order of discussion followed in the preceding two sections, and begin with resource rather than final product prices.

The general scheme of estimating war output in 1939 prices is indicated in Appendix Table II 4; some of the underlying data are presented in Appendix Table II 5. Because data on the components of war output are confidential, no figures are shown in Appendix Table II 4.

Appendix Table II 4

Schematic Presentation of the Measurement of War Output in 1939 Prices
1939, 1940, First Half of 1941; then by Quarters
Mixed Final Product and Resource Prices

1 Total war output, current dollars
2 Nonmunitions (given directly)
3 Munitions & war construction (line 1 — line 2)
4 Total costs, munitions & war construction
    a) Labor (line 3 x line 5 of App. Table II 5)
    b) Capital & enterprise (line 3 x line 6 of App. Table II 5)
    c) Taxes (line 3 x line 7 of App. Table II 5)
5 Price index for labor costs (see text)
6 Price index for capital & enterprise (App. Table II 5, line 10 after seasonal correction)
7 Resource input, 1939 prices
    a) Labor (line 4a ÷ line 5)
    b) Capital & enterprise (line 4b ÷ line 6)
    c) Taxes (1939 ratio of line 3 of App. Table II 5 to sum of lines 1 & 2 of App. Table II 5 multiplied by sum of lines 7a & b)
    d) Total (lines 7a + b + c)
8 Price index for nonmunitions (see text)
9 Nonmunitions, 1939 prices (line 2 ÷ line 8)
10 War output, 1939 prices (lines 7d + 9)

Implicit Price Indexes

11 Taxes (line 4c ÷ line 7c)
12 Munitions & war construction (line 3 ÷ line 7d)
13 Total war output (line 1 ÷ line 10)

An approximate division of war output into nonmunitions, munitions, and war construction has recently been published in *Budget Message of the President;* Washington, 1944 (see table on p. vi). The apportionment used in the calculations here is from the monthly estimates of the War Production Board.

The adjustment of war output for price changes is carried through separately for two components: (aa) nonmunitions; (bb) munitions and war construction. The former, adjusted by final product prices, and the latter by resource price indexes, together yield (cc) a mixed price index of war output (App. Table II 4). Only by further adjustment of the nonmunitions sector (as well as by allowance for depreciation on war construction) do we get (dd) gross and net war output, in 1939 resource prices.

aa Nonmunitions

These comprise military pay; civilian pay (war agencies); subsistence; travel; agricultural exports; other nonmunitions. Apart from pay items, the group is made up largely of consumer type goods, though subject to considerable modification to satisfy military requirements. Indeed, many of the items are purchased off the shelf rather than contracted for. As their close correspondence with civilian type products seems to warrant the application of wholesale price indexes, appropriate ones were chosen from the BLS wholesale price series. Both military and civilian pay were corrected for recent increases in rates of pay.

The index of final product prices for the nonmunitions segment of total war output rises to about 110 by the last quarter of 1941; averages somewhat over 125 in 1942; and rises further to about 145 in 1943.

bb Munitions and war construction

The conversion to 1939 resource prices was effected by the separate deflation of the main components of munitions output in current prices: labor costs and gross profits, the latter in turn divided between returns to capital and enterprise and corporate income and excess profits taxes. The weights assigned these three components of munitions output are determined by the division of gross output in the five industrial groups (oil, gas and metal mining, chemicals and petroleum refining, metal fabrication, and contract construction) that accounted for the bulk of munitions output and war construction in 1942 and 1943 (see App. Table II 5).

i) *The price index for the labor factor* was based on changes in hourly earnings in war manufacturing industries. A weighted index was constructed by dividing aggregate weekly wages actually paid by aggregate weekly wages, assuming 1939 hourly earnings through-

APPENDIX TABLE II 5

Distribution of Costs, Five 'War' Industries

(dollar figures in millions; base year for index, 1939)

	1939	1940	1941			1942				1943			
			1st Half	III	IV	I	II	III	IV	I	II	III	IV
1 Labor costs (wages & salaries)	8,244	10,092	6,901	4,157	4,545	4,931	5,829	6,902	7,529	7,765	8,259	8,403	8,536
2 Capital & enterprise	3,407	4,369	2,597	1,522	1,735	1,394	1,490	1,676	1,916	1,719	1,789	1,853	1,934
3 Taxes	391	1,103	1,575	983	1,146	1,339	1,455	1,450	1,565	1,742	1,840	1,888	2,037
4 Total (1 + 2 + 3)	12,042	15,564	11,073	6,662	7,426	7,664	8,774	10,028	11,010	11,226	11,888	12,144	12,507
5 Ratio of (1) to (4)	.685	.648	.623	.624	.612	.643	.664	.688	.684	.692	.695	.692	.682
6 Ratio of (2) to (4)	.283	.281	.235	.228	.234	.182	.170	.167	.174	.153	.150	.153	.155
7 Ratio of (3) to (4)	.032	.071	.142	.148	.154	.175	.166	.145	.142	.155	.155	.155	.163
8 Index of (2)	100	128	152	179	204	164	175	197	225	202	210	218	227
9 Index of minerals consumption	100	116	128	137	140	141	139	142	148	151	153	156	158
10 Price index for (2) (8 ÷ 9)100	100	110	119	131	146	116	126	139	152	134	137	140	143

The 5 'war' industries comprise metal mining, oil and gas mining, chemical and petroleum refining, metal fabrication, and contract construction.

Data on wages and salaries (labor costs) are from the Department of Commerce (the annual totals through 1942 published in the *Survey of Current Business*, March 1943, Table 16, p. 23). Taxes and net corporate income (before dividends) from *ibid*, Sept. 1943 (Table 6, p. 7) and earlier issues.

Elements in the capital and enterprise total other than net corporate profits (interest, depreciation and depletion, incomes of individual entrepreneurs) are from the Department of Commerce, and are based on annual totals on Internal Revenue Bureau totals and the corporate sample or (for individual entrepreneurs) on the annual totals and monthly payments.

The index of minerals consumption is based on annual totals (1939-42) estimated by G. H. Moore, interpolated by quarters and extrapolated through 1943 by the materials component of the Federal Reserve Board index of industrial production. Moore's unrevised index, used here, differs from that published in *Occasional Paper 18*, March 1944, p. 17, Table 4, by one point in 1941, a difference too slight to warrant recalculation.

out the period (the number of employees multiplied by the average work week, in hours; the product, i.e., weekly man hours, then multiplied by average hourly earnings in 1939) in a group of 44 war industries (BLS employment and earnings series). This gave, in effect, an index of hourly earnings in these 44 industries combined, weighted by current man hours.[20]

The 44 metal, chemical, and rubber industries covered (BLS designations and arranged in ascending order of the percentage increase in average hourly earnings from 1939 to 1942) follow:

1 Communications equipment
2 Rubber tires & inner tubes
3 Blast furnaces, steel works & rolling mills
4 Tractors
5 Stoves, oil burners & heating equipment
6 Plumbers' supplies
7 Wirework
8 Automobiles
9 Textile machinery
10 Machine-tool accessories
11 Washing machines, wringers & dryers, domestic
12 Lighting equipment
13 Chemicals
14 Sewing machines, domestic & industrial
15 Explosives & safety fuses
16 Fabricated structural & ornamental metal work
17 Typewriters
18 Cash registers, adding & calculating machines
19 Machinery & machine-shop products
20 Machine tools
21 Bolts, nuts, washers, rivets

22 Silverware & plated ware
23 Smelting & refining, nonferrous metals
24 Electrical equipment
25 Hardware
26 Rubber goods, other
27 Agricultural machinery, excl. tractors
28 Stamped & enameled ware & galvanizing
29 Aircraft & parts, excl. aircraft engines
30 Steam & hot-water heating apparatus & steam fittings
31 Cutlery & edge tools
32 Clocks & watches
33 Tools, excl. edge tools, machine tools, files & saws
34 Aluminum
35 Car building, electric & steam railroad
36 Radios & phonographs
37 Forgings, iron & steel
38 Alloying & rolling & drawing
39 Ammunition, small arms
40 Shipbuilding
41 Engines & turbines
42 Pumps and pumping equipment
43 Locomotives
44 Aircraft engines

ii) The current *cost of the capital plus enterprise factor* is the sum of corporate net income after taxes, depreciation, entrepreneurial income, interest, and net rents and royalties. To construct a price

[20] Weighting had almost no effect. The weighted and the unweighted indexes almost kept pace during 1939-42; the high wage industries had a slight tendency to expand less rapidly than the relatively low wage industries.

The weighted index was used through the second quarter of 1943. For the remaining two quarters of that year it was extrapolated by the unweighted index for the 44 industries.

index for this component, changing total cost had to be divided by the changing number of units of capital and enterprise. Since it is difficult to find an index of changes in the input of capital and enterprise analogous to man hours of employment, we used the index of the consumption of raw materials of mineral origin prepared at the National Bureau by G. H. Moore.[21] It may reflect with a fair degree of accuracy the utilization of durable capital in war industries—by and large, the biggest metal consumers in both war and peace; but it is quite unrelated to the enterprise or risk element of gross capital or to such elements of management as are not included in labor income. The net increase in the unit return to capital and enterprise, only slightly greater than in the unit return to labor, is not believed to be excessively large and may conceal a sizable downward bias.

iii) *Corporate income and excess profits taxes* have increased enormously since 1939, especially in the industries that have been largely converted to war production. But the increase reflects the needs of the government for more revenue in wartime rather than additional services performed for corporate enterprises. It can of course be argued that under wartime controls of production and distribution the government has assumed most of the risk and many

---

21 See *Occasional Paper 18*. It is a weighted index comprising 9 metals and 10 non-metals:

METALS	NONMETALS
Ferrous	*Fuels*
Steel ingots & castings	Anthracite coal
	Bituminous coal
Nonferrous	Crude petroleum
Aluminum ⎤	Natural gas
Copper ⎟ primary	
Zinc ⎟ & secondary	*Other nonmetals*
Lead ⎦	Portland cement shipments
Tin consumption	Gypsum
Magnesium	Graphite
Antimony consumption	Sand & gravel
Mercury consumption	Crushed limestone
	Sulphur

Experiments with an index of somewhat different composition more closely related to the 5 'war' industries (excluding coal and including rubber, ethyl alcohol, lumber) yielded a similar index. Recalculation did not, therefore, seem warranted.

A seasonal correction had to be introduced into the price index since it reflects the seasonal influences of such elements in the capital and enterprise totals as dividends and interest (see App. Table II 5, line 10).

of the management functions of corporations, particularly of those manufacturing military equipment. But to the extent that this is true, the increase in the real contribution of capital and enterprise is certainly overstated in our estimates; and any allowance for an increase in the real value of services measured by taxes would be offset by a reduction in the real value of the services of capital and enterprise. We have assumed that in 1939 corporate taxes were the monetary equivalent of the federal government's contribution to business activity; and that thereafter such services kept pace with real output, i.e., with deflated labor and capital costs. As a result of applying this assumption, corporate taxes have an implicit price index of about 700 in 1942 and 800 in 1943; and contribute materially to the rise in the implicit price index for total war outlay in those years.

cc The mixed price index

The combination of the final product price index for nonmunitions and of the resource price indexes for munitions and war construction yielded an annual mixed price index of war output for 1939-41 and quarterly indexes beginning with the third quarter of 1941 (App. Table II 6, col. 3). Detailed quarterly calculations did not seem warranted for the period before the third quarter of 1941, partly because prices had changed so little since 1939, but mainly because the war output totals were so small. From 1939 to the third quarter of 1941 quarterly price indexes were, therefore, constructed by graphic interpolation of the annual figures (App. Table II 6, col. 4).

dd War output, in terms of resource input,
      at current and 1939 prices

To make the results obtained so far usable in calculating gross and net war output at the resource input level, two further steps are necessary: to estimate (i) nonmunitions at resource rather than final product prices, (ii) depreciation on war construction, so that all totals for war output can be adjusted to a net basis.

    i) First we translate the nonmunitions component of gross war output (col. 3, identical with col. 6 of App. Table II 6) to resource input at 1939 resource prices. Again we have recourse to the efficiency index used for consumer goods, though the procedure is probably even more arbitrary here. Nevertheless, for the part of nonmunitions output for which an efficiency index can have a meaning (food, and similar civilian type products, as distinct, e.g., from

APPENDIX TABLE II 6

Derivation of Quarterly Gross War Output and Price Index
Mixed Final Products and Resource Prices
1939 to 1941, Second Quarter
(dollar figures in billions)

YEAR & QUARTER	GROSS WAR OUTPUT		IMPLICIT PRICE INDEX (1939 = 100)			GROSS WAR OUTPUT
	Current prices	1939 prices	Annual & Interpolated quarterly	values	Final series	1939 prices
	(1)	(2)	(3)	(4)	(5)	(6)
1939	1.4	1.4	100		100	1.4
I	.3					.3
II	.3					.3
III	.4					.4
IV	.4					.4
1940	2.8	2.5	112		112	2.5
I	.4			103	103	.4
II	.5			108	108	.5
III	.6			110	110	.5
IV	1.2			115	115	1.0
1941	12.8	10.0	128		128	10.0
I	1.9			120	120	1.6
II	2.5			124	124	2.0
III	3.5	2.7	128		128	2.7
IV	4.9	3.7	132		132	3.7
1942	50.3	34.8	144		144	34.8
I	7.2	5.4	133		133	5.4
II	10.8	7.7	140		140	7.7
III	14.8	10.1	147		147	10.1
IV	17.2	11.6	152		152	11.6
1943	81.3	50.9	160		160	50.9
I	18.9	12.2	154		154	12.2
II	20.7	13.1	159		159	13.1
III	20.6	12.8	161		161	12.8
IV	21.0	12.8	164		164	12.8

COLUMN

1 Survey of Current Business, April 1944, p. 13, Table 10, line 4.

2 By application to col. 1 of annual and quarterly price indexes in App. Table II 4.

3 (Col. 1 ÷ col. 2)100.

4 Interpolated graphically on the basis of annual figures. There was no need to interpolate quarterly for 1939 since the indicated quarterly indexes were not sufficiently above or below 100 to affect the values in current prices in the first decimal place.

5 Combination of col. 3 and 4.

6 Col. 2 when given; for all other periods (col. 1 ÷ col 5)100.

Because of rounding, details will not necessarily check.

the services of the armed forces), the efficiency index in Appendix Table II 2 is perhaps the most reasonable approximation that can be made. Its application yields the adjustment in column 5 of Appendix Table II 7; which, in turn permits us to compute gross war output, in terms of resource input at 1939 prices (col. 6).

ii) Depreciation on war construction in current prices is calculated by applying a ratio, based upon an assumed 10-year life and a straight line apportionment, to the cumulated quarterly volume of war construction (cumulated beginning with the first quarter of 1939). Subtraction from column 1 of Appendix Table II 7 yields net war output in current prices (col. 2).

We adjusted the quarterly totals of depreciation on war construction for price changes by the index of construction costs and prices of durable equipment used by the Department of Commerce for the construction and equipment components of private gross capital formation. It undoubtedly understates the level of current costs of war construction relative to 1939, but may approximate fairly well the changing valuation level in the cumulated total of war construction subject to depreciation. In any event, in view of the crude assumptions that have to be made concerning the scope of this category and the life period underlying the depreciation rate, more laborious and specific procedures for price adjustment did not seem warranted.

Net war output in 1939 mixed resource and product prices is the difference between column 3 of Appendix Table II 7 and the quarterly estimates of depreciation on war construction in 1939 prices; in 1939 resource prices it is the difference between column 6 and the latter.

b *In final product prices*
To convert war output to 1939 final product prices, three assumptions were made concerning the relative efficiency of resources in munitions and war construction (see Sec. 3c). Appendix Table II 8 shows a sample calculation based on assumption *a*. The quarterly index in column 1 is by graphic interpolation to annual totals, which allows for a two-thirds rise of the index from 1939 to the first half of 1943, some retardation in the rise from the third quarter of 1941 to the second quarter of 1942; then a more rapid rise, which loses momentum in the second half of 1943.

APPENDIX TABLE II 7

War Output, Resource Input at Current and 1939 Prices
(billions of dollars, seasonally adjusted annual rates)

YEAR & QUARTER	TOTALS CURRENT PRICES Gross	Net	1939 MIXED PRICES Gross	Net	ADJ. OF NONMUNITIONS TO 1939 RESOURCE PRICES	RESOURCE INPUT 1939 RESOURCE PRICES Gross	Net
	(1)	(2)	(3)	(4)	(5)	(6)	(7)
1939	1.4	1.4	1.4	1.4		1.4	1.4
I	1.2	1.2	1.2	1.2		1.2	1.2
II	1.3	1.3	1.3	1.3	No	1.3	1.3
III	1.4	1.4	1.4	1.4		1.4	1.4
IV	1.5	1.5	1.5	1.5	adj.	1.5	1.5
1940	2.8	2.8	2.5	2.5	through	2.5	2.5
I	1.7	1.7	1.7	1.7		1.7	1.7
II	2.0	2.0	1.9	1.9	1940	1.9	1.9
III	2.6	2.5	2.4	2.3		2.4	2.3
IV	4.8	4.7	4.2	4.1		4.2	4.1
1941	12.8	12.5	10.0	9.7	—0.1	9.9	9.6
I	7.7	7.5	6.4	6.2	—0.1	6.3	6.1
II	10.0	9.7	8.1	7.8	—0.1	8.0	7.7
III	13.9	13.6	10.9	10.6	—0.2	10.7	10.4
IV	19.7	19.3	14.9	14.5	—0.2	14.7	14.3
1942	50.3	49.5	34.8	34.0	—0.5	34.3	33.5
I	28.7	28.1	21.6	21.1	—0.3	21.3	20.8
II	43.2	42.5	30.9	30.3	—0.4	30.5	29.9
III	59.1	58.2	40.2	39.4	—0.6	39.6	38.8
IV	70.3	69.1	46.3	45.2	—0.7	45.6	44.5
1943	81.3	79.5	50.9	49.3	—0.7	50.2	48.6
I	75.6	74.1	49.1	47.8	—0.7	48.4	47.1
II	82.9	81.2	52.1	50.6	—0.7	51.4	49.9
III	82.6	80.7	51.3	49.6	—0.7	50.6	48.9
IV	84.0	82.0	51.2	49.4	—0.7	50.5	48.7

COLUMN

1 *Survey of Current Business,* April 1944, p. 12, Table 7, line 4, and p. 13, Table 10, line 4.

2 Col. 1 minus depreciation on war construction, calculated by applying a 10 per cent charge, a fairly crude approximation, to the total of government-financed war construction—the sum of the public construction items listed in Appendix Table II 3, note to col. 1, as excluded because they represent war construction—cumulated quarterly. Only one-half of the given quarter's construction is included in the cumulated total for that quarter. The quarterly depreciation series is then one-tenth of the quarterly war construction total.

3 From col. 1, by applying the price index in col. 5 of App. Table II 6.

4 Col. 3 minus depreciation on war construction (for values in current prices see note to col. 2) adjusted for price changes by the index of construction costs and prices of durable equipment (obtained by dividing the Department of Commerce quarterly totals for the construction and equipment components of gross capital formation in current prices by those in 1939 prices).

The weights of the indexes in columns 1 and 2, based on the approximate proportions of the two components of war output (in 1939 prices in App. Table II 7), are held constant, since otherwise the proportion of nonmunitions in total war output could be calculated. But in general, variations in the proportions are relatively minor in quarterly totals in recent years.

The implicit prices in column 7 are final product prices reflecting the assumed relative efficiency of resources in munitions and war construction. Appendix Table II 9 presents the more important steps in the calculations based upon assumptions b and c. In accordance with the decision to vary the three assumptions only with respect to the level of relative efficiency set for the first half of 1943, and to make them the same with respect to the relative movement of the efficiency level from 1939 to 1943, the quarterly interpolation of the efficiency indexes, as well as the movement of the annual totals, was established along lines similar to those adopted in the calculations based upon assumption a.

Under the three assumptions, the implicit final product prices for munitions and war construction (and hence for war output) could not be relatives of actual prices in terms of 1939 as 100 unless we disregarded differences in the level of efficiency of resource use in war production relative to that in similar industries in peacetime. What are the *temporal* changes in final product prices of war output, if the level of relative efficiency is disregarded, and what would the totals of war output and national product be if adjusted for such price changes over time alone?

Appendix Table II 10 provides the key price index, calculated from averages of the annual price indexes in war output implicit under the three assumptions in terms of 1939 as 100. This annual index is interpolated quarterly, largely again on the basis of the

Notes to Appendix Table II 7 concluded:
COLUMN

5 Based on the assumed efficiency index (see App. Table II 2, col. 3) applied to the nonmunitions part of war output in 1939 prices. To prevent disclosure of the amounts, the nonmunitions component was here calculated as 0.3 of the total war output in col. 3. Thus the entries in col. 5 are equal to 100 [(col. 3 x 0.3) ÷ efficiency index] — (col. 3 x 0.3).

6 Col. 3 *plus* adjustments in col. 5.

7 Col. 4 *plus* adjustments in col. 5.

Because of rounding, details will not necessarily check.

implicit quarterly price indexes under the three assumptions of Appendix Tables II 8 and 9, smoothed to eliminate erratic fluctuations. Column 5 in Appendix Table II 10 is a matter of straight-

APPENDIX TABLE II 8

Sample Calculation of Gross War Output, 1939 Final Product Prices
Quarterly, 1939-1943

Assumption *a*

(dollar figures in billions, seasonally adjusted annual rates)

	RELATIVE EFFICIENCY OF RESOURCES			GROSS WAR OUTPUT			IMPLICIT
YEAR & QUARTER	Munitions & war construction	Non-munitions	Combined	1939 resource prices	1939 final product prices [(3)x(4)]÷100	Current prices	PRICE INDEX [(6)÷(5)]100
	(1)	(2)	(3)	(4)	(5)	(6)	(7)
1939	48	100	61	1.4	0.8	1.35	165
I	48	99	61	1.2	0.7		
II	48	100	61	1.3	0.8		
III	48	100	61	1.4	0.9		
IV	49	101	62	1.5	0.9		
1940	51	102	64	2.5	1.6	2.8	175
I	50	101	63	1.7	1.1		
II	51	102	64	1.9	1.2		
III	51	103	64	2.4	1.5		
IV	52	103	65	4.2	2.7		
1941	56	105	68.5	9.9	6.9	12.8	187
I	54	104	66.5	6.3	4.2		
II	55	105	67.5	8.0	5.4		
III	57	105	69	10.7	7.4		
IV	59	106	71	14.7	10.4		
1942	67	105	76.5	34.3	26.5	50.3	189
I	61	105	72	21.3	15.3		
II	64	105	74	30.5	22.6		
III	69	105	78	39.6	30.9		
IV	74	105	82	45.6	37.4		
1943	83	105	89	50.2	44.6	81.3	182
I	78	105	85	48.4	41.1		
II	82	105	88	51.4	45.2		
III	85	105	90	50.6	45.5		
IV	88	105	92	50.5	46.5		

COLUMN

1 & 2 Assumed, see text. Annual entries are averages of quarterly.

3 (Col. 1 x 0.75) + (col. 2 x 0.25). Annual entries are averages of quarterly.

4 App. Table II 7, col. 6.

5 Annual entries are averages of quarterly.

6 App. Table II 7, col. 1.

7 Underlying calculation in col. 5 carried to two decimal places.

Because of rounding, details will not necessarily check.

forward calculation from column 4 and estimates of gross war output in current prices (App. Table II 7, col. 1).

4 SUMMARY TABLES

Now that we have discussed the measurement of the three major components of national product (wartime concept)—flow of goods

APPENDIX TABLE II 9

Gross War Output, 1939 Final Product Prices, Quarterly, 1939-1943

Assumptions *b* and *c*

(dollar figures in billions, seasonally adjusted annual rates)

YEAR & QUARTER	ASSUMPTION *b*			ASSUMPTION *c*		
	Relative efficiency of resources in war production (1)	Gross war output, 1939 final product prices (2)	Price index implicit in (2) (3)	Relative efficiency of resources in war production (4)	Gross war output, 1939 final product prices (5)	Price index implicit in (5) (6)
1939	72	1.0	138	84	1.1	119
I	72	0.9		83	1.0	
II	72	0.9		83.5	1.1	
III	72	1.0		83.5	1.2	
IV	73	1.1		84.5	1.3	
1940	76	1.9	144	89	2.3	123
I	74	1.3		86	1.5	
II	75	1.4		88	1.7	
III	76	1.8		89.5	2.2	
IV	77.5	3.3		91	3.8	
1941	82	8.2	156	96	9.6	133
I	79	5.0		93	5.9	
II	81	6.5		95	7.6	
III	82.5	8.8		97.5	10.4	
IV	85	12.5		100	14.7	
1942	92	31.9	158	109	37.8	133
I	87	18.5		103	21.9	
II	89	27.1		106	32.3	
III	94	37.2		111	44.0	
IV	98	44.7		116	52.9	
1943	109	54.8	148	129	64.8	126
I	103	49.8		121.5	58.8	
II	107	55.0		127	65.3	
III	111	56.2		131	66.3	
IV	115	58.1		136	68.7	

See notes to Appendix Table II 8.

Col. 1 and 4 correspond to col. 3 of Appendix Table II 8; col. 2 and 5 to col. 5 of Appendix Table II 8; col. 3 and 6 to col. 7 of Appendix Table II 8.

to consumers, nonwar capital formation, and war output—and presented the estimates for each, we are in a position to assemble summary tables covering both these components and the national product totals (App. Tables II 11-14). The entries in these four summary tables are either transcribed from the appendix tables

APPENDIX TABLE II 10

Gross War Output, Adjusted by an Implicit Final Product Price Index for Munitions and War Construction

YEAR & QUARTER	IMPLICIT ANNUAL PRICE INDEX, 1939=100 UNDER ASSUMPTION			AV. IMPLICIT INDEX	GROSS WAR OUTPUT ($ billions, 1939 product prices)
	a	b	c		
	(1)	(2)	(3)	(4)	(5)
1939	100	100	100	100	1.4
I				100	1.2
II				100	1.3
III				100	1.4
IV				100	1.5
1940	106	104	103	104	2.7
I				100	1.7
II				103	1.9
III				105	2.5
IV				109	4.4
1941	113	116	112	113	11.3
I				111	6.9
II				113	8.8
III				114	12.2
IV				115	17.1
1942	115	114	112	114	44.1
I				115	25.0
II				115	37.6
III				113	52.3
IV				112	62.8
1943	110	107	106	108	75.3
I				110	68.7
II				108	76.8
III				107	77.2
IV				106	79.2

COLUMN

1 App. Table II 8, col. 7.

2 App. Table II 9, col. 3.

3 *Ibid.*, col. 6.

4 Average of col. 1-3 in terms of 1939 as 100 interpolated graphically on the basis of quarterly figures for col. 1-3.

5 100(col. 1 of App. Table II 7 ÷ col. 4).

already presented and discussed, or are the sum of the estimates for the components. The one minor point that calls for comment is the calculation of *net* war output in final product prices (App. Table II 14, col. 3-6): as the difference between the entries in the corresponding columns for gross (App. Table II 13, col. 3-6) and depreciation on war construction, as already calculated in Appendix Table II 7 (war output in resource prices). We could recalculate this depreciation item in terms of final output represented by war construction, by basing it on a share of war output, as shown in App. Table II 13. But it is not clear that the results would

APPENDIX TABLE II 11

National Product and Its Components, Wartime Concept
Quarterly, 1939-1943, Current Prices
(billions of dollars, seasonally adjusted annual rates)

YEAR & QUARTER	FLOW OF GOODS TO CONSUMERS	NONWAR CAPITAL FORMATION		WAR OUTPUT		NATIONAL PRODUCT	
		Gross	Net	Gross	Net	Gross (1+2+4)	Net (1+3+5)
	(1)	(2)	(3)	(4)	(5)	(6)	(7)
1939	64.8	13.2	6.0	1.4	1.4	79.4	72.2
I	63.5	12.7	5.5	1.2	1.2	77.4	70.2
II	64.1	11.6	4.4	1.3	1.3	77.0	69.8
III	65.1	12.5	5.3	1.4	1.4	79.0	71.8
IV	66.3	16.1	8.8	1.5	1.5	83.9	76.6
1940	68.8	16.7	9.3	2.8	2.8	88.3	80.9
I	67.7	16.6	9.3	1.7	1.7	86.0	78.7
II	68.1	14.8	7.4	2.0	2.0	84.9	77.5
III	69.0	16.5	9.1	2.6	2.5	88.1	80.6
IV	70.3	18.8	11.3	4.8	4.7	93.9	86.3
1941	77.7	20.9	13.0	12.8	12.5	111.4	103.2
I	74.1	19.3	11.7	7.7	7.5	101.1	93.3
II	76.8	20.8	13.0	10.0	9.7	107.6	99.5
III	80.4	21.4	13.4	13.9	13.6	115.7	107.4
IV	79.5	22.2	14.0	19.7	19.3	121.4	112.8
1942	85.1	8.8	0.1	50.3	49.5	144.2	134.7
I	83.4	14.7	6.2	28.7	28.1	126.8	117.7
II	82.6	11.8	3.1	43.2	42.5	137.6	128.2
III	85.9	5.5	—3.4	59.1	58.2	150.5	140.7
IV	88.5	3.1	—5.9	70.3	69.1	161.9	151.7
1943	94.1	2.7	—6.5	81.3	79.5	178.1	167.1
I	93.4	2.7	—6.3	75.6	74.1	171.7	161.2
II	92.5	1.9	—7.1	82.9	81.2	177.3	166.6
III	94.2	3.4	—5.6	82.6	80.7	180.2	169.3
IV	96.1	3.0	—6.0	84.0	82.0	183.1	172.1

Column 1: App. Table II 2, col. 1; 2: App. Table II 3, col. 1; 3: *ibid.*, col. 2; 4: App. Table II 7, col. 1; 5: *ibid.*, col. 2.

be better approximations than the estimates in Appendix Table II 7; and in view of the smallness of the item and the necessarily arbitrary character of the underlying assumption concerning length of life, the refinement in consistency did not seem to warrant the additional calculations.

APPENDIX TABLE II 12

National Product and Its Components in Terms of Resource Input Wartime Concept, Quarterly, 1939-1943, 1939 Resource Prices (billions of dollars, seasonally adjusted annual rates)

YEAR & QUARTER	FLOW OF GOODS TO CONSUMERS	NONWAR CAPITAL FORMATION		WAR OUTPUT		TOTAL RESOURCE INPUT	
		Gross	Net	Gross	Net	Gross (1+2+4)	Net (1+3+5)
	(1)	(2)	(3)	(4)	(5)	(6)	(7)
1939	64.8	13.2	6.0	1.4	1.4	79.4	72.2
I	64.3	12.7	5.5	1.2	1.2	78.2	71.0
II	64.7	11.6	4.4	1.3	1.3	77.6	70.4
III	64.6	12.5	5.3	1.4	1.4	78.5	71.3
IV	65.3	16.0	8.7	1.5	1.5	82.8	75.5
1940	66.4	16.1	8.7	2.5	2.5	85.0	77.6
I	66.2	16.2	8.9	1.7	1.7	84.1	76.8
II	66.0	14.4	7.0	1.9	1.9	82.3	74.9
III	66.4	16.0	8.6	2.4	2.3	84.8	77.3
IV	67.1	17.9	10.5	4.2	4.1	89.2	81.7
1941	69.5	18.7	11.1	9.9	9.6	98.1	90.2
I	69.5	17.9	10.4	6.3	6.1	93.7	86.0
II	69.9	18.9	11.3	8.0	7.7	96.8	88.9
III	70.8	18.9	11.2	10.7	10.4	100.4	92.4
IV	67.8	19.0	11.2	14.7	14.3	101.5	93.3
1942	66.6	7.2	—1.0	34.3	33.5	108.1	99.1
I	67.7	12.2	4.2	21.3	20.8	101.2	92.7
II	65.1	9.6	1.4	30.5	29.9	105.2	96.4
III	66.5	4.6	—3.7	39.6	38.8	110.7	101.6
IV	66.9	2.6	—5.8	45.6	44.5	115.1	105.6
1943	67.1	2.1	—6.4	50.2	48.6	119.4	109.3
I	67.4	2.1	—6.4	48.4	47.1	117.9	108.1
II	66.0	1.5	—7.0	51.4	49.9	118.9	108.9
III	67.4	2.5	—6.0	50.6	48.9	120.5	110.3
IV	68.0	2.1	—6.4	50.5	48.7	120.6	110.3

Column 1: App. Table II 2, col. 5; 2: App. Table II 3, col. 6; 3: *ibid.*, col. 7; 4: App. Table II 7, col. 6; 5: *ibid.*, col. 7.

APPENDIX TABLE II 13

Gross National Product and Its Components, Wartime Concept
Quarterly, 1939-1943, 1939 Final Product Prices
(billions of dollars, seasonally adjusted annual rates)

YEAR & QUARTER	FLOW OF GOODS TO CONSUMERS (1)	GROSS NONWAR CAPITAL FORMATION (2)	GROSS WAR OUTPUT				GROSS NATIONAL PRODUCT			
			a Under assumption (3)	*b* (4)	*c* (5)	Disregarding level of relative efficiency (6)	Under assumption (1+2+3) (7)	*a* (1+2+4) (8)	*b* (1+2+5) (9)	Disregarding level of relative efficiency *c* (1+2+6) (10)
1939	64.8	13.2	0.8	1.0	1.1	1.4	78.8	79.0	79.1	79.4
I	63.7	12.6	0.7	0.9	1.0	1.2	77.0	77.2	77.3	77.5
II	64.5	11.6	0.8	0.9	1.1	1.3	76.9	77.0	77.2	77.4
III	64.8	12.5	0.9	1.0	1.2	1.4	78.2	78.3	78.5	78.7
IV	65.9	16.1	0.9	1.1	1.3	1.5	82.9	83.1	83.3	83.5
1940	68.0	16.5	1.6	1.9	2.3	2.7	86.1	86.4	86.8	87.2
I	67.1	16.4	1.1	1.3	1.5	1.7	84.6	84.8	85.0	85.2
II	67.4	14.7	1.2	1.4	1.7	1.9	83.3	83.5	83.8	84.0
III	68.2	16.4	1.5	1.8	2.2	2.5	86.1	86.4	86.8	87.1
IV	69.3	18.5	2.7	3.3	3.8	4.4	90.5	91.1	91.6	92.2
1941	72.7	19.6	6.9	8.2	9.6	11.3	99.2	100.5	101.9	103.6
I	72.2	18.6	4.2	5.0	5.9	6.9	95.0	95.8	96.7	97.7
II	73.0	19.8	5.4	6.5	7.6	8.8	98.2	99.3	100.4	101.6
III	74.3	19.9	7.4	8.8	10.4	12.2	101.6	103.0	104.6	106.4
IV	71.4	20.0	10.4	12.5	14.7	17.1	101.8	103.9	106.1	108.5
1942	69.8	7.6	26.5	31.9	37.8	44.1	103.9	109.3	115.2	121.5
I	71.1	12.8	15.3	18.5	21.9	25.0	99.2	102.4	105.8	108.9
II	68.3	10.1	22.6	27.1	32.3	37.6	101.0	105.5	110.7	116.0
III	69.7	4.8	30.9	37.2	44.0	52.3	105.4	111.7	118.5	126.8
IV	70.1	2.7	37.4	44.7	52.9	62.8	110.2	117.5	125.7	135.6
1943	70.3	2.2	44.6	54.8	64.8	75.3	117.1	127.3	137.3	147.8
I	70.6	2.2	41.1	49.8	58.8	68.7	113.9	122.6	131.6	141.5
II	69.1	1.6	45.2	55.0	65.3	76.8	115.9	125.7	136.0	147.5
III	70.6	2.6	45.5	56.2	66.3	77.2	118.7	129.4	139.5	150.4
IV	71.2	2.2	46.5	58.1	68.7	79.2	119.9	131.5	142.1	152.6

COLUMN

App. Table II 2, col. 2.

App. Table II 3, col. 3.

App. Table II 8, col. 5.

COLUMN

4 App. Table II 9, col. 2.

5 *Ibid.*, col. 5.

6 App. Table II 10, col. 5.

Appendix Table II 14

Net National Product and Its Components, Wartime Concept
Quarterly, 1939-1943, 1939 Final Product Prices
(billions of dollars, seasonally adjusted annual rates)

YEAR & QUARTER	FLOW OF GOODS TO CONSUMERS (1)	NET NONWAR CAPITAL FORMATION (2)	NET WAR OUTPUT Under assumption *a* (3)	*b* (4)	*c* (5)	*Disregarding level of relative efficiency* (6)	NET NATIONAL PRODUCT Under assumption *a* (1+2+3) (7)	*b* (1+2+4) (8)	*c* (1+2+5) (9)	*Disregarding level of relative efficiency* (1+2+6) (10)
1939	64.8	6.0	0.8	1.0	1.1	1.4	71.6	71.8	71.9	72.2
I	63.7	5.4	0.7	0.9	1.0	1.2	69.8	70.0	70.1	70.3
II	64.5	4.4	0.8	0.9	1.1	1.3	69.7	69.8	70.0	70.2
III	64.8	5.3	0.9	1.0	1.2	1.4	71.0	71.1	71.3	71.5
IV	65.9	8.8	0.9	1.1	1.3	1.5	75.6	75.8	76.0	76.2
1940	68.0	9.1	1.6	1.9	2.3	2.7	78.7	79.0	79.4	79.8
I	67.1	9.1	1.1	1.3	1.5	1.7	77.3	77.5	77.7	77.9
II	67.4	7.3	1.2	1.4	1.7	1.9	75.9	76.1	76.4	76.6
III	68.2	9.0	1.4	1.7	2.1	2.4	78.6	78.9	79.3	79.6
IV	69.3	11.1	2.6	3.2	3.7	4.3	83.0	83.6	84.1	84.7
1941	72.7	12.0	6.6	7.9	9.3	11.0	91.3	92.6	94.0	95.7
I	72.2	11.1	4.0	4.8	5.7	6.7	87.3	88.1	89.0	90.0
II	73.0	12.2	5.1	6.2	7.3	8.5	90.3	91.4	92.5	93.7
III	74.3	12.2	7.1	8.5	10.1	11.9	93.6	95.0	96.6	98.4
IV	71.4	12.2	10.0	12.1	14.3	16.7	93.6	95.7	97.9	100.3
1942	69.8	—0.6	25.7	31.1	37.0	43.3	94.9	100.3	106.2	112.5
I	71.1	4.8	14.8	18.0	21.4	24.5	90.7	93.9	97.3	100.4
II	68.3	1.9	22.0	26.5	31.7	37.0	92.2	96.7	101.9	107.2
III	69.7	—3.5	30.1	36.4	43.2	51.5	96.3	102.6	109.4	117.7
IV	70.1	—5.7	36.3	43.6	51.8	61.7	100.7	108.0	116.2	126.1
1943	70.3	—6.3	43.0	53.2	63.2	73.7	107.0	117.2	127.2	137.7
I	70.6	—6.3	39.8	48.5	57.5	67.4	104.1	112.8	121.8	131.7
II	69.1	—6.9	43.7	53.5	63.8	75.3	105.9	115.7	126.0	137.5
III	70.6	—5.9	43.8	54.5	64.6	75.5	108.5	119.2	129.3	140.2
IV	71.2	—6.3	44.7	56.3	66.9	77.4	109.6	121.2	131.8	142.3

COLUMN

1 App. Table II 2, col. 2.

2 App. Table II 3, col. 4.

3 App. Table II 13, col. 3 minus the difference between col. 4 and 5 of App. Table II 12.

COLUMN

4 App. Table II 13, col. 4 minus the difference between col. 4 and 5 of App. Table II 12.

5 App. Table II 13, col. 5 minus the difference between col. 4 and 5 of App. Table II 12.

6 App. Table II 13, col. 6 minus the difference between col. 4 and 5 of App. Table II 12.

PART III

National Product in World Wars I and II

1 SIMILARITIES AND DISSIMILARITIES

Every major war has much the same effect on all industrial economies. Unless invaded or bombed, an advanced industrial country
(and some agricultural countries also) markedly increases its output, especially of goods for the armed forces—at least during the
first years of the conflict. As long as the country remains neutral
and in no apparent immediate danger, the free market mechanism
is allowed to operate as usual; and larger exports to the belligerents
create a semblance of prosperity not unlike that of an ordinary
business expansion. As participation nears and war begins, the
shift in production toward war goods is accelerated; productive
resources are more completely mobilized; market mechanisms are
supplemented or replaced by direct governmental controls; and
diversion from peace to war type production reaches a point where,
despite a huge increase in total output, less is available for civilians.

So typical is this pattern that we expect not only the broad movements in national product during both world wars but even changes
in some of its components to be approximately the same, especially
since the United States' position was similar in many respects.

i) Fighting started on the European continent, and this country remained neutral during the first two to three years. The duration of neutrality did not differ much: 33 months in World War I
and 27 months in World War II.

ii) The United States supplied, as long as it was neutral, large
quantities of goods to belligerents, but chiefly to the countries it
eventually joined as an ally. This production stimulated the expansion of the war industries, so that they were ready to expand
still further for the benefit of the United States armed forces upon
its entrance into the conflict.

iii) The wide division of opinion on the question of participation impeded laying plans and a production basis for mobilization.
This delay, marked in both wars, was succeeded by intensive efforts
to catch up, once the die had been cast.

iv) Far from the theaters of combat (except, in this war, for
its outlying territorial possessions), the United States was in an
ideal position to serve as an arsenal for democracy.

v) But this very distance made the transportation of troops and
equipment a bottleneck; and the physical and spiritual remoteness
became, after a while, a barrier to economic mobilization at heavy
cost to civilians.

To select the aspects of dissimilarity between the two wars of large import for the productive performance of this country's economy is more difficult. The vicissitudes of historical experience during twenty-five years inevitably create important dissimilarities. Some of the outstanding ones between World Wars I and II are listed below.

vi) Perhaps the chief difference lies in the fact that World War I occurred after six to seven decades during which major wars were conspicuous by their absence, and World War II occurred only a quarter of a century after World War I. This meant that the nation entered this war with some experience in dealing with the economic problems a war raises (e.g., price control, inflation, and international trade). It meant also a vital difference in the structure of the world economic and social organization.

vii) This war came shortly after the most acute economic depression (1929-32) the industrial nations had experienced since 1870 (or perhaps earlier); and followed another marked depression (1937-38). Though World War I followed the depression of 1907-08 and two 'submerged' business cycles—1908-11 and 1911-14 —the preceding decade was not so distorted by violent depressions.

viii) The imminence of participation in the conflict was felt more keenly in this country in 1940-41 than in 1914-16. Small as the defense effort that began in July 1940 seems in retrospect and in comparison with the record in 1942 and 1943, it was distinctly bigger (even relatively) than that before 1917.

ix) The United States has long been among the industrially advanced countries of the world. But its relative industrialization and industrial power were perhaps further ahead of others (especially its adversaries) in 1939 than in 1914. Its industrial structure had suffered less from the devastation of World War I, and it led other countries in industrial expansion during the 1920's.

x) The fortunes of the first years of the war created a more serious military and economic problem for this country than in 1917. In addition, the new character of the armed conflict made ever greater demands upon the economy, especially upon industries manufacturing highly fabricated metal products.

xi) The country's active participation in this war had, on February 7, 1945, been twice as long (38 months) as in World War I.

2 TIMING OF COMPARISON AND BASE YEARS

In drawing comparisons between the two wars, what specific years or quarters should be set off against each other or used as bases? Should we compare data for 1914 and for 1939, the years in which war broke out on the European continent; and should we, therefore, measure changes in output from 1914 and 1939 as bases? Or should we take into account the fact that 1914 was a year of depression and 1939 a year of recovery; and, therefore, measure output during each war from the base of the preceding cyclical peak year, 1913 and 1937 respectively?

As our aim is to establish the similarities and differences in the movement of national product and its components attributable to the wars, the first year of World War I is compared with the first year of World War II; the second year with the second year, and so on. Similarly, the choice of the base year is governed by the war chronology. As our interest lies in the progress of output from the time each war started, the base years must be 1914 and 1939. The differences in their cyclical characteristics should, of course, not be forgotten when the indexes for which they are bases are interpreted. But since many other elements of dissimilarity must also be taken into account, it seems better to select base years with reference to the indisputable formal chronology of the war than to make a difficult and never absolutely certain choice of prewar bases completely comparable as to cyclical and other characteristics.

Our record for this war, analyzed in greater detail in Part II, extends only through 1943. At the time of writing, detailed estimates for 1944 were not available. In 1914-18 and 1939-43 we have two equal periods, but the former covers the full span of a war, and unfortunately World War II is not yet over. Hence, any conclusions concerning the greater relative extent of the war effort and its effects on the size and distribution of national product in World War II would most probably be strengthened were the record of this war complete.

3 MOVEMENT OF GROSS NATIONAL PRODUCT (WARTIME CONCEPT)

According to our analysis in Part I, the total output of an economy in wartime is most adequately measured by national product gross of the consumption of durable capital and of all war goods (Tables III 1 and 2).

TABLE III 1

Gross National Product, Wartime Concept, World Wars I and II
(dollar figures in billions)

WORLD WAR I

	1914	1915	1916	1917	1918
1 Gross national product, current prices	36.3	39.8	45.6	57.5	64.3
2 Price indexes (1914 = 100)					
a) Over-all implicit	100	102	110	132	155
b) Cost of living, BLS	100	101	108	128	150
c) Wholesale prices, BLS	100	102	126	173	193
3 Gross national product, 1914 prices	36.3	39.2	41.3	43.7	41.6

WORLD WAR II

	1939	1940	1941	1942	1943
4 Gross national product, current prices	79.4	88.3	111.4	144.2	178.1
5 Price indexes (1939 = 100)					
a) Resource prices	100	104	114	133	149
b) Final product prices, assumption *b*	101	102	111	132	140
c) Cost of living, BLS	100	101	106	117	124
d) Wholesale prices, BLS	100	102	113	128	134
6 Gross national product, 1939 prices					
a) Resource input	79.4	85.0	98.1	108.1	119.4
b) Final product, assumption *b*	79.0	86.4	100.5	109.3	127.3

LINE	LINE
1 App. Table III 1, line 9.	4 Table II 1, line 4a.
2a App. Table III 4, line 5.	5a & b Table II 3, line 4, and Table II 4, line 5b.
3 App. Table III 6, line 3.	6a & b Table II 5, lines V 1 and 2b.

a *In current prices*

The totals in current prices, naturally, do not have to be adjusted for price changes and differentials in war years; and, while the estimates for World War I are much cruder and subject to a wider margin of error than those for this war, the main conclusions may be accepted as fairly reliable.[1] For the five years covered for each

[1] The propriety of the *approach* used here to estimate gross national product (wartime concept) for World War I is tested in Appendix Table III 3. Since the payments-savings approach yields for recent years totals fairly close to those computed by other methods, no large error can be attributed to it. However, for the earlier years, the estimates of income payments and business savings are cruder.

As in Part II, the estimates of gross national product and other aggregates used here differ from those already published by the National Bureau in that they exclude imputed rent and net savings of governments (see comparison for 1919-21 in App. III, comments on App. Tables III 1-3). These departures were made to assure comparability with the Department of Commerce estimates for the years beginning with 1939.

war, the rate of increase in gross national product (wartime concept) in current prices is appreciably higher in World War II (Table III 2, lines 3 and 6). Comparisons based on rough quarterly interpolations, for a period beginning with the quarter immediately preceding the outbreak of each war in Europe and ending with the last quarter within each war covered by available data (lines 9 and 12), confirm this greater rise in the annual totals.

In both wars the rise was accelerated by this country's entrance: the rate of increase was much higher during its active participation than during its neutrality and incipient belligerency. In this war the

TABLE III 2

Gross National Product, Wartime Concept, Percentage Changes
World Wars I and II

| | | PERCENTAGE CHANGE PER QUARTER IN | | |
	NUMBER OF QUARTERS	Gross national product, current prices	Over-all price indexes	Gross national product, constant prices
A ANNUAL ESTIMATES				
World War I				
1 1914 to 1916	8	2.9	1.2	1.6
2 1916 to 1918	8	4.4	4.4	0.1
3 1914 to 1918	16	3.6	2.8	0.9
World War II				
4 1939 to 1941	8	4.3	1.2	3.1
5 1941 to 1943	8	6.0	2.9	3.0
6 1939 to 1943	16	5.2	2.1	3.0
B QUARTERLY ESTIMATES				
World War I				
7 1914-II to 1917-I	11	3.0	1.8	1.2
8 1917-I to 1918-IV	7	3.7	4.4	—0.6
9 1914-II to 1918-IV	18	3.3	2.8	0.5
World War II				
10 1939-II to 1941-IV	10	4.7	1.6	3.0
11 1941-IV to 1943-IV	8	5.3	2.2	3.0
12 1939-II to 1943-IV	18	4.9	1.9	3.0

For World War I: based on Table III 1 and App. Tables III 7 and 8.

For World War II: based on Table III 1 and App. Tables II 11 and 13. The calculations here are based on line 5b of Table III 1 and the corresponding totals in constant prices.

rate during both neutrality and participation was close to one and a half times the rate for World War I.

b *Price levels*

For recent years we can adjust, at least roughly, for both changes over time and differentials in prices between the war and nonwar sectors. As similar data are not available for World War I, prices in the war sector must be based directly upon those in private markets. However, since prices in private markets were restricted much less, the failure to apply rigid price controls to munitions and war construction, for reasons justified by the urgency of military demand, may not have caused the marked disparity in pricing bases between the war and nonwar sectors that seems to have characterized recent years.

In general, constructing a price index for the war sector during World War I entailed attributing crude weights to the various categories of war output and assigning to them appropriate price indexes (App. Table III 4). For recent years the price index most comparable with the earlier period is that based upon assumption *b:* namely, that by the first half of 1943 the efficiency of war production, relative to efficiency in other sectors of the economy, was the same as in 1939, but that it was stepped up from 1939 to 1943. As this index probably understates the price level of war output relative to the price level in the nonwar sectors, both war output and gross national product in constant prices are correspondingly overstated. But a similar bias is likely to characterize the prices used to adjust war output and gross national product to constant prices in World War I.

For purposes of *comparison,* the indexes in Table III 1, lines 2a and 5b, seem most satisfactory.[2] The rise in the price level was ap-

[2] The relation between these indexes and such commonly used measures as the BLS cost of living and wholesale price indexes is different in the two wars. In World War I the index implicit in national product is somewhat higher than the cost of living index but appreciably lower than that of wholesale prices. In 1942 and 1943 it is appreciably higher than the cost of living index and higher than the wholesale price index.

The difference is due largely to the fact that, while in both wars the prices of finished munitions and war construction were probably not subject to strict supervision, in recent years there has been more price control in the nonwar sector.

A comparison of price indexes implicit in gross national product with the most comprehensive measures of movement in the compensation of labor in the two wars confirms the similarities and differences revealed by Table III 1 (see App. Table III 5).

preciably less in World War II. This conclusion would be the same were we to use the customary cost of living and wholesale price indexes. In both wars the rate accelerated markedly from the period of neutrality to that of participation, as is evident from the annual estimates for 1914-18 and from the calculations based upon quarterly estimates. For World War II it is definitely due to our specially designed price measures for war output and the greater weight of war output in national product. However, even the BLS indexes show the acceleration, at least when annual totals are compared (Table III 1, lines 5c and d).

During neutrality preceding both wars prices rose at about the same rate. The chief difference occurred during participation. It was in the years following the country's entrance into this war that prices were held down appreciably more than in 1917 and 1918.

c In constant prices

Differences during the two wars between the movements of national product in current prices and the rates at which the price indexes rise cause marked differences in the movement of national product in constant prices (Table III 2, last column). During World War II national product in constant prices, both annual totals and quarterly approximations, increased at a rate over three times as high as during World War I.

During the period of neutrality preceding World War I the rate was much higher than during participation. The slight rise in the annual totals from 1916 to 1918 was negligible compared with almost 2 per cent per quarter from 1914 to 1916. Quarterly totals rose substantially per quarter during the eleven quarters preceding the entrance of the country into World War I, but declined slightly during the seven quarters of participation.

During participation in this war, on the contrary, national product in constant prices rose as much per quarter as during the two years of neutrality. This sustained rise indicated by the annual totals is confirmed by the quarterly estimates when we compare the eight quarters from the end of 1941 to the end of 1943 with the preceding ten quarters, from the middle of 1939 to the end of 1941. The rate of rise is much higher in this war than in World War I during neutrality; and the difference is even greater during participation.

These conclusions would not be modified if price changes were adjusted for by the customary price indexes. The estimates of national product in constant prices for World War I would be about the same, but those for World War II would rise even faster than those in Table III 2.

The better performance of the productive system in this war can be explained partly by the greater preparation for war production during the period of neutrality (Sec. III 4):[3] the base upon which to expand war production was wider and some experience had been accumulated in ways of steering clear of the acute dislocations that hindered the expansion of output in World War I.

The second and probably more important factor was the relatively large stock of unused resources in this country at the beginning of World War II in Europe, and as late as 1941; in 1914, and especially in early 1917, the situation was much tighter. In 1939 national product in constant prices was only slightly larger than in 1929, whereas population had increased almost 9 per cent during the decade and net capital accumulation was taking place, even if at a lower rate than during the 1920's.[4] In 1914 and 1916 national income in constant prices was appreciably larger than in 1904 or 1906.[5]

[3] This appears to be true even if we take into account exports of war goods, interpreted broadly to include not only fully finished (airplanes and parts, explosives, firearms) but also the more important mixed product categories (aluminum, brass, copper, nickel and zinc products, automobiles and parts, electrical machinery, tires, engines, rails). From slightly over $100 million in the year ending June 30, 1914 exports rose to $1.5 billion in the year ending June 30, 1917 (to decline to $0.7 billion in the next fiscal year). At their peak they were 3 per cent of gross national product (see App. Table III 7). Together with direct war output, they amounted, before this country entered World War I, to about 4 per cent of gross national product. In 1941 the share of *direct* war output was 11.5 per cent (see Table III 3).

[4] National income in current prices, as measured by the Department of Commerce, increased 10 per cent from 1938 to 1939; and the cost of living index declined $1\frac{1}{2}$ per cent. If we assume that national product in constant prices increased roughly 12 per cent from 1938 to 1939, the total for 1939 (in 1929 prices) would be $88 billion (see Simon Kuznets, *National Income and Its Composition*, I, Table 5, p. 147). The corresponding total for 1929 was $87 billion. For the increase in population and net capital formation in 1929-38, see *ibid.*, Table 8, p. 151, and Table 39, p. 276.

[5] Robert F. Martin's totals of realized private production income, when adjusted for price changes by the cost of living index, rise 32 per cent from 1904 to 1914; 35 per cent, from 1906 to 1916 (see his *National Income in the United States, 1799-1938*, National Industrial Conference Board, 1939, Table 3, pp. 14-5). Regardless of the margin of error in the current price totals and in their adjustment by the cost of living index, the suggested 30 per cent rise during the decade preceding World War I is in sharp contrast to the at most 1 or 2 per cent rise during the decade preceding World War II.

In 1939 unemployment was estimated to be 10.4 million, almost one-fifth of the labor force; by the end of 1941 it was still 4 million (the average for the year was 5.6 million). There is no evidence of such extensive unemployment in this country in 1914, and it was probably less in 1916 and early 1917.[6]

Another related factor was the lower level of average working hours in 1939 than in 1914. In manufacturing, actual weekly hours of work per wage earner were 51 in 1914 and 38 in 1939 (see Solomon Fabricant, *Employment in Manufacturing, 1899-1939,* National Bureau of Economic Research, 1942, Table C-1, col. d, p. 234); and there were probably equally sizable reductions in working hours in other industries. It was, therefore, possible in recent years to raise the intensity of utilization of the *employed* labor force by a much greater relative percentage than could have been done during World War I.

Finally, there was greater awareness of what World War II would entail, more readiness to plan ahead and to adopt promptly whatever course seemed necessary to reorient the economy to the pressing needs of a global military conflict. This, together with idle resources and the fairly large war output attained during neutrality, was a big factor in the remarkable expansion of war and total output after December 7, 1941.[7]

[6] For annual estimates of unemployment and the labor force for recent years see the *Survey of Current Business,* April 1943, Table 1, p. 10. For monthly data for 1940 and 1941 see *ibid.,* June 1943, Table 9, p. 30.

For World War I relevant data appear in *Recent Economic Changes* (National Bureau of Economic Research, 1928), II, Table 29, p. 468, and Table 37, p. 478. Applying to the entries in Table 29 the upward adjustment suggested by Table 37, we get total unemployment for 1914 of roughly 3 million, or about 8 per cent of the labor force; and for 1916 of at most 1 million, or about 2½ per cent. In 1939 and 1941 unemployment was almost 20 and 10 per cent of the labor force.

The results are roughly similar if we extrapolate the estimates of minimum unemployment in the above-cited Table 37 by Paul Douglas' estimates of unemployment in mining, manufacturing, transportation, and the building trades (see his *Real Wages in the United States, 1890-1926,* Houghton Mifflin, 1930, Table 172, p. 460). This extrapolation (including an adjustment of the figures in *Recent Economic Changes* for an underestimate of unemployment due to a slight undercount of the total gainfully occupied as compared with W. I. King's later figures in *National Income and Its Purchasing Power,* National Bureau of Economic Research, 1930) yields an unemployment total of 2.7 million in 1914; 1.1 in 1916 and 1917; and 1.0 in 1918.

[7] Once the hesitation and dislocation that characterized the winter of 1917-18 particularly had been overcome, national product might well have increased substantially had World War I continued.

4 WAR AND NONWAR COMPONENTS

a *Share of the war component*

Through most of the five years, and especially during participation, the increase in war output was an important source of the increase in national product. We therefore begin the analysis of the composition of national product by studying the share of its war component, i.e., of war output of various descriptions, dominated by munitions (Table III 3).

TABLE III 3

War Output as a Percentage of Gross National Product

Wartime Concept, World Wars I and II

WORLD WAR I

Based on Annual Estimates	1914	1915	1916	1917	1918
1 In current prices	0.8	0.8	1.1	10.6	25.7
2 In 1914 prices	0.8	0.8	1.0	9.4	23.3
Based on Estimates for Selected Quarters[1]					
3 In current prices				1.0	31.4
4 In 1914 prices				0.9	28.6

WORLD WAR II

Based on Annual Estimates	1939	1940	1941	1942	1943
5 In current prices	1.8	3.2	11.5	34.9	45.6
6 In 1939 prices	1.3	2.2	8.2	29.2	43.0
Based on Estimates for Selected Quarters[2]					
7 In current prices	1.7		16.2		45.9
8 In 1939 prices	1.2		12.0		44.2

For World War I: based on App. Tables III 7 and 8.
For World War II: based on App. Tables II 11 and 13.

[1] II for 1914; I for 1917; IV for 1918.   [2] II for 1939; IV for 1941; IV for 1943.

Until this country entered World War I, the share of war output in national product was relatively small. Even in the first quarter of 1917, just before the declaration of war, it was only 1 per cent; and could not be raised above 4 per cent even by a generous allowance for exports to allies. Though it increased rapidly, it was somewhat less than one-third at its peak, in the last quarter of 1918. Annual and quarterly estimates, in both current and 1914 prices, all give the same impression.

The record for World War II is markedly different in two respects. First, the share of war output increased appreciably even before December 1941. For example, the annual totals in 1939 prices rose from somewhat over 1 per cent in 1939 to 8 per cent in 1941; the quarterly data indicate a bigger increase—to 12 per cent by the last quarter of 1941. Second, by the end of 1943 war output constituted a much larger share, 44 per cent, of national product than at the peak of World War I, 29 per cent.

Apparently both the preparatory stages and the years of active participation in this conflict were characterized by relatively greater mobilization of the productive system for war than in World War I.[8] This difference is obviously both cause and effect of the difference discussed in Section III 3: the larger rise in national product in constant prices in this war. Because war output was larger, gross national product was larger; consequently, a bigger share of it could be devoted to war purposes.

b *Changes in war and nonwar sectors*
War output can be expanded by diverting resources ordinarily used for civilian purposes, by more intensive utilization of resources, by putting idle ones to work, or by a combination of all. Table III 4 summarizes changes in the war and nonwar sectors of national

[8] The relative engagement for war purposes of various productive factors, e.g., labor, cannot be compared, even roughly. A War Department estimate of 9.4 million in war work in World War I (see the *Annual Report of the Secretary of War, 1919*) is not confirmed by detailed evidence; and, if the term is equivalent to munitions and related industries as defined in recent years, the estimate is patently too high.

However, the extent of mobilization into the armed forces and federal war agencies can be compared. At the time of the Armistice, the armed forces in World War I were at their peak—4.1-4.2 million; with the addition of those who had lost their lives, close to 4.3 million (J. M. Clark, *The Costs of the World War to the American People,* Yale University Press, 1931, p. 34). On January 1, 1919 the gainfully occupied were estimated to be 40.8 million (W. I. King, *National Income and Its Purchasing Power,* p. 47). The percentage in the armed forces was, therefore, slightly over 10. In January 1944 the armed forces were estimated to be 10.4 million; the labor force, 60.9; yielding a ratio of over 17 per cent (see *Survey of Current Business,* Jan. 1944, Table 2, p. 2).

Inclusion of an allowance for the federal war agencies raises the percentage for World War II more than that for World War I. According to W. I. King the number attached to the federal government, excluding the army, navy, marine, and postal service, did not increase much more than 0.2 million (*op. cit.,* p. 361). In World War II federal war agencies account for 1.5 million (*Survey of Current Business,* Jan. 1944, Table 2, p. 2). The percentage of the gainfully occupied in the armed forces and war agencies was 11 at the peak of World War I; 19, at the end of 1943.

product, compares them with changes in the total, and establishes the relative movement in the nonwar sector. The percentage increase in war output does not admit of meaningful comparisons since the base from which it starts is so low in each period.

During the neutrality interval preceding this war, both national product and the sum of its two nonwar components increased more than before World War I. But war output also increased—accounting for one-third of the increase in national product. For World War I the increase is almost exclusively in the flow of consumer goods and nonwar capital formation. The absolute rise in war output is small. In other words, the addition to national product before this war can be roughly attributed two-thirds to the nonwar and one-third to the war sector; and before World War I, 98 and 2 per cent respectively.

The differences between current experience in active participation and that of World War I are even wider. Since national product failed to increase, and if anything, declined slightly during World War I, the large absolute expansion in war output took place completely at the expense of the nonwar sector. The estimates are crude but indicate that the nonwar sector declined about one-fifth to one-third during the 19 months of this country's participation in World War I. As between the two components of the nonwar sector (App. Table III 6) the decline was much greater in capital formation—by 1918 to one-fifth of the level in 1916; but consumers' outlay also declined—roughly 6 per cent. These declines, in constant prices, are about the same as those in recent quarters.[9]

As during active participation in this war gross national product increased substantially, war production could feed not only upon the diversion of resources from nonwar but also upon an increase in the total amount and productivity of resources used. Slightly over one-half of the increase in the war sector was accounted for by an increase in national product, and less than one-half by a decline in the volume of resources devoted to nonwar production (Table III 4).

The two wars are, therefore, fairly similar in the extent to which nonwar output was reduced under the pressure of participation in

---

[9] Not much importance can be attributed to the fact that the percentage decline in the nonwar sector was somewhat greater in World War I (Table III 4): the quarterly estimates, which alone show this difference, are too crude for it to be taken into account.

TABLE III 4

War and Nonwar Components of Gross National Product
Wartime Concept, Changes, World Wars I and II
(dollar figures in billions)

WORLD WAR I

	1914 to 1916	1916 to 1918	1914-II to 1917-I	1917-I to 1918-IV
A *Totals, Current Prices*				
1 Change in war component	+0.2	+16.0	+0.2	+20.1
2 Change in nonwar component	+9.1	+2.7	+13.9	—5.2
3 Change in gross national product	+9.3	+18.7	+14.1	+14.9
4 % (1) is of (3)	2.0	85.6	1.4	
B *Totals, 1914 Prices*				
5 Change in war component	+0.1	+9.3	+0.1	+11.2
6 Change in nonwar component	+4.9	—9.0	+5.1	—13.0
7 Change in gross national product	+5.0	+0.3	+5.2	—1.8
8 % (5) is of (7)	2.0		1.9	
9 % change in nonwar component	+13.6	—22.0	+13.9	—31.0

WORLD WAR II

	1939 to 1941	1941 to 1943	1939-II to 1941-IV	1941-IV to 1943-IV
A *Totals, Current Prices*				
1 Change in war component	+11.4	+68.5	+18.4	+64.3
2 Change in nonwar component	+20.6	—1.8	+26.0	—2.6
3 Change in gross national product	+32.0	+66.7	+44.4	+61.7
4 % (1) is of (3)	35.6		41.4	
B *Totals, 1939 Prices*				
5 Change in war component	+7.2	+46.6	+11.6	+45.6
6 Change in nonwar component	+14.3	—19.8	+15.3	—18.0
7 Change in gross national product	+21.5	+26.8	+26.9	+27.6
8 % (5) is of (7)	33.5		43.1	
9 % change in nonwar component	+18.3	—21.5	+20.1	—19.7

For World War I: based on App. Tables III 7 and 8.
For World War II: based on App. Tables II 11 and 13.

the armed conflict. However, there is a marked difference in the source of war output; and naturally the much longer duration of this war means a greater cumulative effect of the reduction in nonwar output.

5 CHANGES IN INDUSTRIAL COMPOSITION

a *In current prices*

Data are not available on the industrial distribution of gross na-

tional product (wartime concept), but changes in its origin by
major industrial divisions are not likely to differ much from those
in the industrial distribution of the income payments-business savings aggregate (Table III 5).

TABLE III 5

Income Payments-Business Savings Aggregate
Percentage Distribution by Industrial Categories
World Wars I and II
(based on totals in current prices)

WORLD WAR I

		1914	1915	1916	1917	1918
1	Agriculture	12.7	12.6	12.7	15.0	17.4
2	Mining	2.7	2.8	3.4	3.0	3.0
3	Manufacturing	18.8	20.4	25.4	24.8	24.0
4	Contract construction	4.3	4.2	4.0	2.5	2.2
	Commodity production $(1 + 2 + 3 + 4)$	38.5	40.0	45.5	45.3	46.6
5	Transportation (excl. motor)	8.3	8.1	7.7	6.9	8.0
6	Other public utilities	1.3	1.3	1.2	1.1	1.2
7	Trade	13.7	12.8	11.9	14.5	12.3
	Transportation & trade $(5 + 6 + 7)$	23.3	22.2	20.8	22.5	21.5
8	Service & miscellaneous (excl. gov.)	31.8	31.7	28.6	26.6	21.2
9	Government	6.3	6.0	5.1	5.6	10.8
	All services $(8 + 9)$	38.1	37.7	33.7	32.2	32.0

Based on App. Table III 9.

WORLD WAR II

A	Major Categories	1939	1940	1941	1942	1943
1	Agriculture	7.4	6.8	7.6	9.1	9.5
2	Mining	1.9	2.0	2.0	1.8	1.7
3	Manufacturing	24.0	26.1	29.4	30.7	32.5
4	Contract construction	2.7	2.8	3.7	4.7	2.9
	Commodity production $(1 + 2 + 3 + 4)$	36.0	37.7	42.7	46.3	46.6
5	Transportation	7.0	6.9	6.6	6.7	6.5
6	Other public utilities	3.4	3.3	2.7	2.2	1.9
7	Trade	15.5	15.6	15.3	13.1	11.8
	Transportation & trade $(5 + 6 + 7)$	25.9	25.8	24.6	22.0	20.2
8	Service & miscellaneous (excl. gov.)	24.1	23.2	20.7	18.3	16.3
9	Government	14.1	13.3	11.8	13.5	17.0
	All services $(8 + 9)$	38.2	36.5	32.5	31.8	33.3

B	Minor Categories					
	MANUFACTURING					
1	Food, beverages, & tobacco	3.4	3.2	3.0	2.7	2.5
2	Paper, printing, & publishing	2.4	2.4	2.3	1.8	1.7
3	Textiles & leather	3.8	3.7	4.1	3.7	3.4
4	Construction materials & furniture	2.2	2.3	2.5	2.2	1.9
5	Chemicals & petroleum refining	2.1	2.3	2.5	2.4	2.4
6	Machinery, transportation equipment, & other metal products	8.9	10.9	13.7	16.4	19.1
7	Miscellaneous & rubber	1.2	1.2	1.4	1.4	1.5

Table III 5 concluded:
B *Minor Categories (concl.)*

	1939	1940	1941	1942	1943
TRADE					
1 Wholesale	5.4	5.4	5.4	4.6	4.1
2 Retail	10.1	10.2	9.9	8.4	7.7
GOVERNMENT					
1 Federal	7.3	6.9	6.6	9.3	13.4
2 State & local (incl. public education)	6.8	6.4	5.2	4.2	3.5
SERVICE & MISCELLANEOUS					
1 Finance	9.6	9.0	7.9	6.9	6.2
2 Service & miscellaneous	14.5	14.2	12.8	11.4	10.1

Based on Department of Commerce estimates, *Survey of Current Business*, April 1944, p. 15, Table 16.

Many of the changes in the industrial distributions of the totals in current prices are similar in the two wars. Agriculture accounts for an increasing share, the percentages rising more or less consistently during the five years covered and their relative increase being roughly the same. The share of mining rises in the earlier years of both wars, then declines. The shares of transportation, other public utilities, trade, and service and miscellaneous (excluding government) decline. The share of government declines during both neutrality periods, and rises markedly during participation.

The big difference between the two wars is in construction. By 1918 its share, which had declined steadily, was down to one-half of the 1914 percentage. From 1939 to 1942 it rose markedly, declining only in 1943.

Data on minor industrial categories are available only for recent years; but the behavior of their shares in World War I was probably similar. The increase in the share of total manufacturing is due primarily to the large increase in the share of the machinery, transportation equipment, and other metal products group, which includes most of the munitions industries. Of the other manufacturing groups, only chemicals and petroleum refining, and miscellaneous and rubber also account for increasing shares of the income payments-business savings aggregate. In contrast, the purely consumer goods industries—food, beverages, and tobacco; paper, printing, and publishing; and even textiles and leather—account for declining shares. In trade the shares of both the wholesale and the retail divisions decline. In government the decline of the share to 1941 and the rise thereafter is accounted for by the movement of income originating in the federal government; the share of state and local government, including public education, declines steadily. In the service and miscellaneous group, the two categories distinguished—finance, and service and miscellaneous—account for declining shares.

Changes in the industrial distribution of the income payments-business savings aggregate in current prices are not too reliable a measure of changes in the industrial composition of national product in real terms. Prices of final products or of resources for the several product and industry categories move at different rates during the periods characterized by the general price rise associated with a war. For example, in both wars prices of farm products rose at a higher rate than the over-all price index; whereas prices of nonfarm products rose less than the general price level.[10] In transportation and public utilities, in which charges are relatively inflexible, the rise in prices was bound to be less than in industries whose products are not as subject to fixed schedules. We must, therefore, attempt to establish whether, when adjusted for differences in price movements among various categories of final products or resources, the shares of the several industrial divisions would change as those in current prices do in Table III 5.

b *Employed labor force*
Changes in the distribution of total employment (including self-employed and family labor) roughly approximate those in the industrial composition of national product in real terms. Though the former do not take into account possible interindustry differences in the relative use of capital per person engaged, in the utilization of the employed labor force (measured, e.g., by man hours), or in the skill composition of the labor force, it is the only other over-all measure co-extensive in scope with national product in current prices (Table III 6).

Showing elements of similarity in the two wars, these distributions confirm some of the relative shifts in the distributions of the income payments-business savings aggregate. The share of manufacturing increases; the shares of trade and of the service and mis-

---

10 For World War I see F. C. Mills, *Economic Tendencies in the United States* (National Bureau of Economic Research, 1932), particularly pp. 205-20. For World War II see his 'Prices in a War Economy', *Occasional Paper 12*, Oct. 1943, particularly Table 5, p. 19.

cellaneous category decline; and the share of government increases, especially after this country entered the wars.

But there are three marked differences between changes in the industrial composition of the employed labor force and in the industrial distribution of the income payments-business savings aggregate (Table III 5). First, in contrast to an increase in the share of total income payments and savings originating in agriculture, the share of the labor force employed in agriculture declines, somewhat more in World War II than in World War I. In other words, the relatively greater wartime inflation of prices of farm products may have been the main source of the increase during both wars in the

TABLE III 6
Total Employed Labor Force
Percentage Distribution by Industrial Categories
World Wars I and II

A WORLD WAR I

		1914	1915	1916	1917	1918
1	Agriculture	23.1	22.9	21.7	21.5	21.2
2	Mining	3.2	3.0	3.0	3.0	2.9
3	Manufacturing	20.7	20.6	23.0	24.3	25.0
4	Construction	3.3	3.1	3.1	2.8	2.3
	Commodity production (1 + 2 + 3 + 4)	50.2	49.6	50.8	51.6	51.4
5	Transportation & public utilities	7.5	7.2	7.2	7.4	7.7
6	Trade	10.8	11.0	10.8	10.7	10.4
	Transportation, public utilities, & trade (5 + 6)	18.3	18.2	18.0	18.2	18.1
7	Government	5.2	5.3	5.2	6.8	12.8
8	Service & miscellaneous	26.3	26.9	26.0	23.4	17.7
	All services (7 + 8)	31.5	32.2	31.2	30.2	30.5

Based on App. Table III 10, Part A.

B WORLD WAR II

		1939	1940	1941	1942	1943
1	Agriculture	20.6	19.8	17.0	15.3	13.5
2	Mining	1.9	2.0	1.9	1.8	1.5
3	Manufacturing	22.5	23.3	25.8	27.0	27.9
4	Construction	4.5	4.3	4.9	4.2	2.5
	Commodity production (1 + 2 + 3 + 4)	49.6	49.4	49.7	48.4	45.4
5	Transportation & public utilities	6.7	6.7	6.6	6.3	6.1
6	Trade	17.5	17.6	16.8	15.2	13.5
	Transportation, public utilities, & trade (5 + 6)	24.2	24.2	23.4	21.5	19.6
7	Government	9.6	10.1	12.1	16.7	24.1
8	Service & miscellaneous	16.6	16.3	14.8	13.5	11.0
	All services (7 + 8)	26.2	26.3	26.9	30.2	35.1

Based on App. Table III 10. In Part A, but not in Part B, employees are reduced to full-time equivalents. Government includes employees of government owned and operated arsenals and shipyards.

share of agriculture in the income payments-business savings aggregate in current prices.

Second, in contrast to the marked decline in the share of transportation and public utilities in the income payments-business savings aggregate, its share in the employed labor force is maintained in both wars with the exception of the decline in 1942 and 1943 (which is due largely to the marked increase in the total because of additions to the armed forces). The failure of the prices of transportation and other utility services to rise as much as the general price level accounts for their smaller share in the income payments-business savings aggregate; though these industries continued to contribute proportionately as much, if not more, to national product in real terms.

Third, the share of government in the payments-savings aggregate increases in both wars but not until after this country's entrance; even then, the absolute increase is not large (from 6.3 per cent in 1914 to 10.8 per cent in 1918; and from 14.1 per cent in 1939 to 17.0 per cent in 1943). But of the total labor force, including the armed services, government claims a steadily mounting share in both wars, especially upon the mobilization of the armed forces: from 5.2 per cent in 1914 to 12.8 per cent in 1918; and from 9.6 per cent in 1939 to 24.1 per cent in 1943. Obviously, it is the relatively low remuneration of the armed forces that prevents as big a rise in the government's share in the income payments-business savings aggregate as in its share in the total labor force.

c *Shares of selected industries, adjusted for differential price changes*
Absence of accurate data precludes making a separate adjustment for price changes in the net value product (i.e., the income payments-net business savings total) originating in each industry. Adjusted figures can be approximated, however, by means of indexes of physical output for some of the industries listed in Tables III 5 and 6. For both wars, measures of physical output, free from the distorting effects of price changes, are at hand for agriculture, mining, manufacturing, construction, and the major part of transportation. A comparison of these indexes with the movement of gross national product in constant prices shows whether output in these industries increased more or less during each period than national product in real terms. The ratio of the index of physical output in a

given industry to the index of gross national product in constant prices (the base years for both being 1914 and 1939 respectively) can then be applied to the share of the given industry in the income payments-business savings aggregate in current prices for 1914 and for 1939; and shares of these industries in national product in real terms approximated for subsequent years.

TABLE III 7

Percentage Shares of Selected Industries in National Product
Constant Prices, World Wars I and II

	WORLD WAR I	1914	1915	1916	1917	1918
1	Agriculture	12.7	11.8	10.2	10.2	11.2
2	Mining	2.7	2.7	3.0	3.0	3.1
3	Manufacturing	18.8	20.4	22.9	21.6	22.4
4	Contract construction	4.3	3.5	3.4	3.3	3.5
5	Transportation	8.3	8.2	9.0	9.4	10.3
	WORLD WAR II	1939	1940	1941	1942	1943
6	Agriculture	7.4	7.0	6.2	6.3	5.6
7	Mining	1.9	1.9	1.8	1.7	1.5
8	Manufacturing	24.0	25.5	29.1	33.7	35.3
9	Contract construction	2.7	2.8	3.6	3.7	1.7
10	Transportation	7.0	6.9	7.4	8.6	8.8

Based upon applying to the percentages for 1914 and 1939 respectively (from Tables III 5A and B) the ratios calculated by dividing the indexes of physical output for each industry by the index of gross national product in constant prices (App. Table III 11).

The percentages in Table III 7, calculated in this fashion, confirm the evidence of Tables III 5 and 6. The share of agriculture in national product (both numerator and denominator in constant prices) shrinks markedly in both wars, indicating that agricultural output did not increase nearly as much as total output. In World War II the share of mining declines, appreciably only after the country is well along in active participation, because an expansion in raw material production must precede that in finished war goods. In World War I, on the contrary, it increases fairly continuously.[11] The share of manufacturing gains substantially in both wars, but not after 1916 in World War I, and much more steadily and ap-

[11] The evidence concerning the movement of the shares of mining in the two wars (Tables III 6 and 7) is contradictory, owing perhaps to inadequacy of the employment estimates and of the physical output indexes. Conclusions concerning this industrial category are, therefore, omitted from further discussion.

preciably in World War II.[12] Detailed data for this war indicate that the increase is due to the increases in industries most actively engaged in producing war implements. The share of construction declines in World War I and increases during World War II through 1942. Its drop in 1943 is due obviously to the completion of the expansion of facilities that precedes maximum production of finished war goods. The share of transportation increases in both wars, owing to the heavier burden placed upon the transportation system by the demands of expanded war production and the greater movement of both goods and men.

The similarities noted in the shifts in the industrial composition of national product can perhaps be explained in terms of persisting differences in the expansibility of the several industries in response to war needs; in the extent to which war needs mean bigger demand for their products; in the ease with which their prices can be controlled; in the degree to which other means of compulsion can be exercised by public authorities to mobilize resources. These factors serve to explain why agriculture accounts for an increasing share of the income payments-business savings aggregate and a declining share of national product in real terms, why the share of manufacturing in national product in both current and constant prices increases, and why public utilities account for a declining share in current prices and a mounting share in constant prices.

The differences in the changes in industrial composition—the chief of which, as mentioned, is in the share of construction—are associated with other differences noted in Sections 3 and 4: the greater increase in national product in World War II and the bigger share in it of war output. In recent years the country has had huge stocks of resources to draw on in extending old facilities and building up an impressive number of new ones for the specific purposes

[12] The index for World War I, originally constructed by W. W. Stewart and recently revised by Solomon Fabricant (*Employment in Manufacturing, 1899-1939: An Analysis of Its Relation to the Volume of Production,* National Bureau of Economic Research, 1942, p. 331), is more heavily weighted with industrial materials and semifabricates than the Federal Reserve Board index, used for recent years, which is heavily weighted with man hour series for war industries. Consequently, when we compare them, manufacturing is shown to have risen more during recent years relatively to World War I than if both indexes were equally biased by being overweighted with industrial materials and semifabricates or with man hour series. It may be doubted, however, that the differential bias in the two indexes is so great as to cancel the much greater rise in the share of manufacturing during World War II (Table III 7).

of war production. During the period of neutrality preceding World War I, in contrast, construction was kept down by competitive market pressures; its possible expansion after this country entered the war was restrained by the tightness of resources which made it impossible to produce war goods on a huge scale and increase construction at the same time. In World War II the greater increase in war output is associated also with the greater increase in the share of manufacturing in total national product.

6 Distribution by Type of Income or Payment

a *Gross national product*

Aggregate income payments, including entrepreneurial savings, alone can be allocated by type of payment. The other components of gross national product, as defined and estimated here—net profits retained by corporations, additions to tax payments, and charges for depreciation and depletion—are not income flows to individuals from economic enterprises. However, before studying changes in the composition of income payments by type, we consider this aggregate and view the flow to individual income recipients as part of gross national product, the most comprehensive measure of total output (Table III 8).

TABLE III 8

Gross National Product, Wartime Concept (unadjusted for inventory revaluation), Percentage Distribution among Income Payments and Other Components, World Wars I and II (based on totals in current prices)

World War I

		1914	1915	1916	1917	1918
1	Income payments, incl. entrepreneurial savings	91.2	88.7	86.4	84.3	87.0
2	Corporate savings	0.6	3.5	6.2	6.0	1.8
3	Additions to corporate income & profits taxes	0	0	0.2	3.5	4.7
4	Depreciation & depletion	8.3	7.8	7.0	6.3	6.6
5	Gross product, unadj.	100.0	100.0	100.0	100.0	100.0

World War II

		1939	1940	1941	1942	1943
6	Income payments, incl. entrepreneurial savings	88.7	87.5	86.0	84.7	83.5
7	Corporate savings	2.4	3.8	5.4	4.4	3.7
8	Additions to corporate income & profits taxes	0	0.3	1.4	4.2	6.5
9	Depreciation & depletion	9.0	8.4	7.2	6.7	6.3
10	Gross product, unadj.	100.0	100.0	100.0	100.0	100.0

For World War I, calculations based upon Appendix Table III 1, lines 1, 2, 3, 5, 6, and 7; for World War II, upon Appendix Table III 3, lines 1, 2, 3, 4, and 5.

There is close similarity in the distributions of the unadjusted gross national product totals among income payments and other items.[13] In both wars the proportion accounted for by income payments is close to 90 per cent in the early years, then declines, but by relatively minor percentages. The share of corporate savings increases markedly during the two intervals of neutrality, and stays on a level above that of prewar years even during participation. The additions to corporate income and profits taxes, caused largely by the bigger needs of government in connection with war output, naturally account for the increase in their share of gross national product—a share almost the same in the two wars. Depreciation and depletion, which rises much more slowly than national product in current prices, accounts for declining shares, the declines also being about the same in the two wars.

The amount distributed in income payments to individuals constitutes merely a fraction, though a preponderant one, of national product. That this fraction shrinks in wartime is natural: a progressively larger proportion of the nation's output is bought, and is intended to be bought, by a purchaser other than individual income recipients, i.e., the government. Indeed, were income payments to individuals geared closely to the value of product the economic system makes available for individuals' purchases in wartime, the ratio of income payments to gross national product would have been much lower than in Table III 8; and would have declined much more from the first to the last year in the two periods covered. It does not because spendable incomes of individuals (as distinct from incomes received) are reduced by higher taxes as well as by borrowing—the two methods by which government gets the share of individuals' income payments needed to finance the part of gross national product not available for consumers' purchases or private investment. To the degree that these two methods, especially taxation, are effective, the distribution of income payments by type does not have as much meaning in wartime as in peacetime, since it does not approximate as well the true net compensation of the productive factors involved. No adjustment can be made, because it is impossible to determine how much the government gets by taxes

13 Since for World War I inventory revaluation cannot be apportioned between savings of corporations and of individual entrepreneurs, we have to use totals unadjusted for it.

or borrowing from each type of payment. But the qualification must be borne in mind in subsequent analysis.

b *Payments by type*

Shifts in the distributions of income payments by type in the two wars are similar in many respects (Table III 9). The parallel shifts are clearer in Table III 10. All types, except employee compensation and dividends, move similarly not only during both wars but also

TABLE III 9

Aggregate Payments, including Entrepreneurial Savings
Percentage Distribution by Type, World Wars I and II
(based on totals in current prices)

A WORLD WAR I

		1914	1915	1916	1917	1918
1	Employee compensation	55.1	53.9	52.5	49.5	55.7
2	Entrepreneurial net income					
	a) Agriculture	10.2	10.6	11.3	13.7	15.3
	b) Other	15.3	16.6	16.6	19.0	12.6
	c) Total	25.5	27.2	27.9	32.7	27.9
3	Service income (1 + 2c)	80.6	81.1	80.4	82.2	83.6
4	Dividends	6.0	5.7	7.8	7.3	6.2
5	Interest	4.4	4.5	3.9	3.5	3.5
6	Rent	9.0	8.8	7.9	7.0	6.7
7	Property income (4 + 5 + 6)	19.4	19.0	19.6	17.8	16.4
8	Total payments (3 + 7)	100.0	100.0	100.0	100.0	100.0
9	Corporate savings as % of total payments	0.7	3.9	7.3	7.0	2.1

Based on App. Table III 9.

B WORLD WAR II

		1939	1940	1941	1942	1943
10	Employee compensation	68.3	69.0	69.5	71.5	73.6
11	Entrepreneurial net income					
	a) Agriculture	6.1	5.8	6.8	8.3	8.6
	b) Other	9.7	10.1	10.3	9.3	8.1
	c) Total	15.8	15.8	17.1	17.6	16.7
12	Service income (10 + 11c)	84.1	84.8	86.6	89.1	90.3
13	Dividends	5.4	5.3	4.9	3.4	2.8
14	Interest	7.2	6.8	5.7	4.7	4.2
15	Net rents & royalties	3.3	3.1	3.0	2.9	2.7
16	Property income	15.9	15.2	13.6	11.0	9.7
17	Total payments (12 + 16)	100.0	100.0	100.0	100.0	100.0
18	Corporate savings as % of total payments	0.6	2.4	4.3	3.8	3.4

Based on Department of Commerce estimates in *Survey of Current Business*, April 1944, Table 15, p. 15.

during neutrality and participation. For example, the share of the net income of entrepreneurs in agriculture increases during both intervals of neutrality, and even more during belligerency; that of entrepreneurs in other industries increases during both intervals of neutrality, and declines during belligerency in both wars (although the movement in World War I is quite erratic). The share of service incomes, i.e., employee compensation plus entrepreneurial net income, which represents payments largely for direct services by individuals, increases somewhat more during World War II. This means that the share of property income—dividends, interest, and

TABLE III 10

Percentage Shares of Various Types of Payment and of Corporate Savings in Aggregate Income Payments Changes, World Wars I and II

WORLD WAR I

		1914-16	1916-18	1914-18
1	Employee compensation	—2.6	+3.2	+0.6
2	Entrepreneurial net income			
	a) Agriculture	+1.1	+4.0	+5.1
	b) Other	+1.3	—4.0	—2.7
	c) Total	+2.4	0	+2.4
3	Service income (1 + 2c)	—0.2	+3.2	+3.0
4	Dividends	+1.8	—1.6	+0.2
5	Interest	—0.5	—0.4	—0.9
6	Rent	—1.1	—1.2	—2.3
7	Property income (4 + 5 + 6)	+0.2	—3.2	—3.0
8	Total payments (3 + 7)	0	0	0
9	Corporate savings as % of total payments	+6.6	—5.2	+1.4

WORLD WAR II

		1939-41	1941-43	1939-43
10	Employee compensation	+1.2	+4.1	+5.3
11	Entrepreneurial net income			
	a) Agriculture	+0.7	+1.8	+2.5
	b) Other	+0.6	—2.2	—1.6
	c) Total	+1.3	—0.4	+0.9
12	Service income (10 + 11c)	+2.5	+3.7	+6.2
13	Dividends	—0.5	—2.1	—2.6
14	Interest	—1.5	—1.5	—3.0
15	Net rents & royalties	—0.3	—0.3	—0.6
16	Property income	—2.3	—3.9	—6.2
17	Total payments (12 + 16)	0	0	0
18	Corporate savings as % of total payments	+3.7	—0.9	+2.8

Based on Table III 9.

rents and royalties combined—must decline. The shares of interest and rent decline in both wars and periods. Finally, corporate savings, as a percentage of total payments, also rise during both intervals of neutrality and decline during belligerency.

The two exceptions characterize the period of neutrality: the share of employee compensation declines during the interval of neutrality before World War I, and increases from 1916 to 1918; it increases from 1939 to 1941, and even more from 1941 to 1943. The share of dividends increases during the interval of neutrality before World War I, and declines from 1916 to 1918; it declines from 1939 to 1941, and even more from 1941 to 1943, so that, by the end of 1943, it is one-half of its prewar level.

The similarities are expected. When prices are rising and effort is directed to commodity production, shares of such relatively fixed types of payment as interest and rent naturally decline; the share of farmers' net income increases with the rise in the share of agriculture in national product in current prices. In years of neutrality, i.e., when business is prosperous and not burdened by heavy taxes, corporate savings constitute a mounting percentage of income payments; when participation in a war brings higher taxes, it constitutes a declining percentage.

The differing movements in the share of dividends can perhaps best be explained by the difference in the impact of direct taxes upon the members of the community of whose total income dividends constitute a large proportion. Since dividends are concentrated in the upper income brackets, a high income tax, and especially surtax rates, will impede dividend distributions, while low tax rates will further it. As high normal and surtax rates did not go into effect early in World War I, they did not begin to influence incomes until 1917. Also, during World War I the individual received a credit for dividends in his *normal* tax base; this meant a smaller differential burden on income paid out as compared with that retained by the corporation than now, when dividends are fully taxed. High even for incomes in 1939, the normal and surtax rates were raised for 1940, so that corporations had less incentive to increase dividend disbursements proportionately to their net profits. Moreover, benefiting from experience with the consequences of a major war in their bearing upon the obsolescence of capital investment and needs for funds for postwar reconversion, corporations have followed a more conservative policy in this war than they did in World War I.

The difference in the movement of the share of employee compensation during the intervals of neutrality is less easy to explain. One would expect that, in general, as was the case during the 1920's, a business expansion such as took place from 1914 to 1916 would be accompanied by a rise in the proportion employee compensation constituted of total income payments. That this was not the case in 1914-16 may be due to the rise in dividends and entrepreneurial net income. During the neutrality interval before World War I, the share of entrepreneurial net income increased more than before World War II (Table III 10, col. 1). As dividends also were increasing relatively more than total income, the *share* of employee compensation would not increase as much, and might even decline.

7 DISTRIBUTION BY SIZE

Wartime reduction in unemployment and shifts in the distribution of income payments by type are among the factors that should effect changes in the distribution of income among recipient or population groups at various income levels. Do the upper income brackets receive an increasing or decreasing share of total income payments? Is the distribution of income by size more or less concentrated?

Important as these questions are, no data are available for accurate answers; and useful as distributions of income flows among recipients or among population groups at various income levels would be for economic analysis and policy, they cannot be made on a fully adequate basis even for recent years, let alone for World War I. However, a few estimates that indicate relations are presented.[14]

For World War I two types of measure are available, both for the distribution at relatively high income levels (Table III 11). The first, showing the percentage of total income going to the highest 5 per cent of income recipients (line 1), suggests that during

[14] All are in current prices, before any tax deductions. For purposes of measuring changes in the distribution of spendable incomes among various recipient groups, we would obviously need to adjust for changes in the tax load and for differential changes in the cost of living among income groups. Neither adjustment is possible; and the fact that we deal with total income payments in current prices, rather than with spendable income adjusted for price differentials among various income groups, must be kept in mind in interpreting the estimates discussed below.

the interval of neutrality it rose somewhat, but that during participation it declined markedly.

The second compares the income of the recipient group above a given dollar level with the income of recipients below (lines 2 and

TABLE III 11

Measure of Changes in the Distribution of Income by Size

World War I

	1914	1915	1916	1917	1918
1 % of total income received by highest 5% of income recipients	32	31	34	29	25
2 Ratio of av. income per person in group over $2,000 to av. in group under $2,000	10.8	7.7	7.8	5.6	4.7
3 (2) divided by ratio of $2,000 to av. income per recipient	5.0	3.8	4.3	3.7	3.5
4 Ratio of av. income per person in group over $5,000 to av. in group under $5,000 (both in 1913 prices)	16.9	20.2	20.6	16.8	14.2
5 (4) divided by ratio of $5,000 to av. income per recipient (both in 1913 prices)	3.2	3.9	4.2	3.4	2.8
6 Ratio of weighted av. deviation to av. realized income per gainfully occupied	0.20	0.18	0.12	0.10	0.09

LINE

1 See *Income in the United States* (National Bureau of Economic Research, 1922), II, p. 334, Table 26D.

2 Derived from *ibid.*, p. 332, Table 26C. Entries are a ratio of (a) (% of income in the over $2,000 group) ÷ (% of recipients in the over $2,000 group) to (b) (% of income in the under $2,000 group) ÷ (% of recipients in the under $2,000 group).

3 For total income paid out and number of recipients used to derive the average income per recipient see *ibid.*, p. 331, Table 26A.

4 Basic data from W. I. King, *National Income and Its Purchasing Power* (National Bureau of Economic Research, 1930), Table XXXII, p. 173, and Table XXXIII, p. 178. For method of calculation see note to line 2.

5 Average income in 1913 prices calculated from the tables cited in the note to line 4.

6 Based on the distribution of the gainfully occupied and of realized income (excl. the miscellaneous category) (W. I. King, *op. cit.*, Table III, p. 53, and Table XIV, pp. 94-5) by industries—agriculture, mining, manufacturing, construction, transportation, trade, banking, government, and unclassified.

The average deviation is computed by (a) subtracting from 1 the ratio of the % of income to the % of gainfully occupied in each industrial division; (b) multiplying the item under (a) for each industrial division by its % of gainfully occupied; (c) adding the products under (b), disregarding sign; (d) dividing the sum under (c) by 100. The result of (d) is entered directly in line 6, since the average income per gainfully occupied, implicit in the whole calculation, is 1.

4). Such measures, by themselves, do not reveal changes in the distribution, since as the average income per recipient rises or falls, the meaning of a fixed dollar level as an indicator of relative income status changes. For example, $5,000 exceeded the average income in 1914 much more than in 1918. We must, therefore, adjust the distribution based upon dividing lines drawn at a fixed dollar level by the ratio of this level to the average for all income recipients. While this adjustment is crude, lines 3 and 5 are much more reliable measures of changes in relative dispersion than lines 2 and 4.

The measure based upon the dividing line at $5,000 (in 1913 prices) shows, like line 1, that the percentage of incomes going to the upper brackets rose from 1914 to 1916 and dropped markedly from 1916 to 1918. The measure based upon the dividing line at $2,000, on the contrary, shows that the percentage declined during neutrality; but, as in lines 2, 4, and 5, the decline during participation was steeper. Like the first measure, these two indicate that during the interval of neutrality the distribution of incomes remained the same or became more dispersed, and during participation tended more nearly to approach equality.

No direct evidence is available for World War I on the distribution of income by size among the vast body of income recipients below these few upper brackets. Circumstantial evidence, however, suggests that it must have become less dispersed. The reduction in unemployment meant fewer potential income recipients whose incomes were zero or close to it, i.e., cutting off the extreme left-hand tail of an income distribution constructed (as it should be) for all income recipients, potential and actual. Also, interindustry shifts tended on the whole to raise the average level of incomes in the industries that, before the war, were well below the average (line 6). The increase in agricultural income per capita was a large factor in reducing the contribution of interindustry differences in income per gainfully occupied to the dispersion of the income distribution.

For World War II the data are somewhat richer, yet far from comprehensive and conclusive. Like line 1 of Table III 11, Table III 12 measures changes in the percentage of total income going to upper income recipients, but it covers also dependents instead of recipients alone. The percentage of income received by the upper 10, 7, 4, 3, and even 2 per cent declined from 1939 to 1941. In contrast, the percentage of income received by the upper 1 per cent showed no significant decline (top panel). If the ratios in the lowest panel were plotted, the Lorenz curve would be more concave in 1940

TABLE III 12

Percentage of Total Income Received by a Given Percentage of the Total Population (incl. Farmers) with the Highest Per Capita Incomes, 1939-1941

	10%	7%	4%	3%	2%	1%
1939	33.64	27.29	20.51	18.19	15.35	11.53
1940	31.54	26.33	20.33	18.08	15.34	11.66
1941	30.70*	25.38*	19.79	17.53	14.88	11.34

	SUCCESSIVE DIFFERENCES				
	10-7%	7-4%	4-3%	3-2%	2-1%
1939	6.35	6.78	2.32	2.84	3.82
1940	5.21	6.00	2.25	2.74	3.68
1941	5.32	5.59	2.26	2.65	3.54

RATIO OF SHARE OF INCOME TO SHARE OF POPULATION WITHIN THE UPPER 10%					
	10-7%	10-4%	10-3%	10-2%	10-1%	Full 10%
1939	0.63	0.65	0.66	0.68	0.73	1.00
1940	0.55	0.59	0.61	0.64	0.70	1.00
1941	0.58	0.59	0.61	0.64	0.70	1.00

*Or 30.88 for 10% of population and 25.42 for 7% when all returns under $3,000 are combined.

The number of persons dependent upon the income reported in *Statistics of Income* on individual and taxable fiduciary returns with net income is cumulated downward from the highest net income group by $1,000 net income groups and its percentage of the total population as of July 1 (Bureau of the Census) computed.

Total income is likewise cumulated and expressed as percentages of income payments to individuals (*Survey of Current Business*, April and August 1944).

The percentage of income received by a given percentage of the population is then based on the interpolations to the logarithms of cumulated population and income.

The number of persons dependent upon the income reported in *Statistics of Income* is the sum of the number of returns (joint returns are given double weight) and the number of dependents (total credit for dependents, as reported, divided by the per capita allowance).

In the calculations above, total income as reported in *Statistics of Income* is adjusted by subtracting capital gain, net gain from sales of property other than capital assets, and business and partnership losses.

For 1939 and 1940, for net income groups of $5,000 and over, partly tax exempt interest received on government obligations as reported on the face of the return is replaced by total interest received as reported in the information schedule of the return.

For 1941, data for returns on Form 1040A are distributed by net income groups on the basis of the distribution of returns on Form 1040 up to $3,000.

and 1941 than in 1939. This suggests that with narrower dispersion from 1939 to 1941 between the top income group and the mass of income recipients, there was increased dispersion in the distribution within the top group proper.[15]

For 1941-43 distributions comparable with the distribution of income among consuming units in 1935-36, published originally by the National Resources Planning Board, have been prepared. A summary (Table III 13) indicates that dispersion diminished from 1935-36 to 1941, and that this tendency continued, though it was slighter, to 1943.

TABLE III 13

Shares of Lowest and Highest Tenth and Three-tenths
in Total Income, 1935-1936 and 1941-1943

Families	1935-36	1941	1942	1943
1 Share of lowest tenth	1.3	1.4	1.4	1.5
2 Share of lowest three-tenths	7.9	8.2	8.4	8.6
3 Share of highest tenth	38.4	36.1	35.3	34.2
4 Share of highest three-tenths	64.4	63.0	62.3	61.4
5 Coefficient of variation	1.49	1.28	1.17	1.08
Single Consumers				
6 Share of lowest tenth	1.5	1.6	1.6	1.6
7 Share of lowest three-tenths	9.2	9.4	9.6	9.7
8 Share of highest tenth	32.9	31.5	31.0	30.4
9 Share of highest three-tenths	60.4	59.5	59.1	58.7
10 Coefficient of variation	1.24	1.08	1.08	1.03

Estimates for 1941-43 are for the distribution of civilian money income alone, excluding imputed value of farm products retained for home consumption, wages and relief in kind; and excluding payments to military personnel and institutional residents. For 1935-36 a comparable estimate was derived.

The distributions underlying the calculations above were prepared by Hildegarde Kneeland and William G. Madow in the Office of Price Administration, Division of Economic Research.

The increase in the percentage of income received by the lowest one-tenth and the lowest three-tenths of the family and individual consumer groups indicates a similar tendency at the other end of the income scale between 1941 and 1943. Whether this was true also between 1939 and 1941 is a matter for conjecture. But here again indirect evidence of the type already cited in connection with

15 Again we must note that the distributions are for total income, i.e., do not take account of income tax deductions.

World War I—the reduction in unemployment and the greater rise in per capita income in industries with below-the-average per capita income, such as agriculture—suggests that it was.

The similarities and differences between the two wars are in harmony with those in changes in the distribution of income payments by type. Obviously, a decline in the share of property incomes, particularly of dividends and interest, would, other conditions being equal, mean a decline in the proportion of income received by the upper income brackets. As stated in Section 5, the share of property incomes, particularly of dividends, declined steadily from 1939 through 1943; consequently, a smaller percentage of total income was received by the very high income groups. In World War I the share of property incomes, particularly of dividends, declined only between 1916 and 1918. From 1914 to 1916, on the contrary, the share of dividends increased. There is a parallel movement in the size distribution of income, again between the high income brackets and the mass of income recipients: the distribution remained the same or became more dispersed from 1914 to 1916; from 1916 to 1918, dispersion narrowed.

8 SUMMARY

By way of summary, a conspectus of similarities and differences in the movement of national product and of its components during the two wars is presented in Table III 14. It notes merely the chief parallels and deviations from them, and states the conclusions without the qualifications emphasized in the text.

One aspect of these conclusions that cannot be recorded in the tabular summary deserves special comment: the interrelation of the movements of national product and its components, in both their similarities and their differences during the two wars. There was obviously a close connection between the rise in national product in real terms stimulated by the wars, the increasing proportion in it of war output, and the gains in the shares of manufacturing and transportation. Likewise, there was a definite interconnection among the differences in the movement of national product: between its smaller gain and the lower level reached by the share of war output in World War I, the smaller share of war output, the smaller gain in

TABLE III 14

Conspectus of Similarities and Differences in the Movement
of Gross National Product and Various Components
World Wars I and II

SIMILARITIES	DIFFERENCES
I GROSS NATIONAL PRODUCT	
1 *In Current Prices*	
Appreciable rise; at much higher rates during participation than during neutrality.	The rate in World War II almost 1½ times that in I, both for the period as a whole & during neutrality & belligerency.
2 *Price Levels*	
Rise; at much higher rates during participation than during neutrality.	Rise greater in World War I than in II, the chief difference being during participation.
3 *In Constant Prices*	
Appreciable rise.	The rate during World War II over 3 times as high as during I. The difference is especially marked for the periods of participation: in World War I the rise was negligible; in II it continued through belligerency at about the same rate as during neutrality.
II SHARE OF WAR OUTPUT (constant prices)	
Appreciable rise.	World War I peak 29% (1918), II, 44% (1943).
Rise especially rapid & great after this country entered the war.	During the neutrality interval preceding World War I it scarcely rose & remained minor until the day of entry. In II it rose to 10% before entry.
No corresponding similarity.	In World War II the increase in war output, even after entry, fed to a large extent upon a rise in national product. In I it was associated almost exclusively with a decline in the nonwar sector.
III CHANGES IN THE NONWAR SECTOR (SUM OF CONSUMERS' OUTLAY & NONWAR CAPITAL FORMATION) (constant prices)	
Appreciable rise during neutrality.	Rise somewhat greater in neutrality interval preceding World War II than in I.
Decline, especially in nonwar capital formation, during participation.	No corresponding difference.
IV INDUSTRIAL COMPOSITION	
1 *Shares in Income Payments-Business Savings Aggregate* (*current prices*)	
Shares of agriculture & mfg. rose; transp., other public utilities, trade, & service & misc. declined. Share of gov. declined during neutrality & rose during participation.	In World War I share of contract construction declined; it rose 1939-42 & declined in 1943.

2 *Shares in Employed Labor Force* (*incl. self-employed & armed forces*)

Shares of agriculture, trade, & service & misc. declined; mfg., transp. & other public utilities, & gov. rose, the last especially during participation.

The decline in share of agriculture & the rise in share of mfg. greater in World War II than in I.

3 *Shares in National Product* (*constant prices*)

Share of agriculture declined; of mfg. & transp. rose appreciably.

Share of construction declined in World War I; rose 1939-42, & declined in 1943. Relative rises in share of mfg. & declines in share of agriculture bigger in World War II.

V DISTRIBUTION OF INCOME BY TYPE (current prices)

1 *Shares in Gross National Product*

Share of aggregate income payments, about 90% of gross national product, declined 4-5%.

No corresponding difference.

2 *Shares in Aggregate Income Payments*

a PROPERTY AND SERVICE INCOME

Shares of interest, rent, & property income declined; of total service income rose.

Decline in share of property income & rise in that of service income larger in World War II, especially in neutrality, though shift in favor of service income not as marked as during participation.

b ENTREPRENEURIAL NET INCOME

Share of net income of agricultural entrepreneurs rose; of entrepreneurs in other industries rose during neutrality, declined during participation.

No corresponding difference.

c EMPLOYEE COMPENSATION AND DIVIDENDS

No corresponding similarity.

Decline in share of employee compensation & rise in share of dividends before World War I offset by respective rise & decline during participation. In World War II former rose & latter declined consistently.

d RATIO OF CORPORATE SAVINGS TO AGGREGATE INCOME PAYMENTS

Rose, especially during neutrality, though there was some offsetting decline during participation.

At 1943 peak only ½ of 1916-17 peak.

VI DISTRIBUTION OF INCOME BY SIZE

1 *Extreme Upper Range*

Share in total income declined.

In World War II share declined continuously; in I, rose during neutrality & declined greatly during participation.

2 *Below Extreme Upper Range*

Reduction in unemployment & relatively greater rise in low income yielding industries, especially agriculture, than in high income yielding industries probably caused a more even distribution of income, though lack of data precludes definite conclusions for World War I.

No corresponding difference.

the share of manufacturing, and the absence of an advance in the share of construction.

With respect to the monetary income flows and their distribution by type of payment or by size, there was again a connection between the increase in the share of service incomes and the changing proportion of income going to the very high income groups and to the mass of lower income recipients. These changes were fairly similar in the two wars. Again the differences are interrelated: the decline in the share of wages and salaries during the neutrality interval preceding World War I, the gain in the share of dividends, and the tendency toward wider dispersion in the distribution by size —none of these being observed during the neutrality interval preceding World War II. This reasonable and expected close interrelation of the movements in various components of national product or national income lends our conclusions, as to both the similarities and differences during the two wars, a weight they would not have in its absence.

We must end as we began—by calling attention to the difference in the periods compared: though equal in length, 1914-18 covers all World War I, but 1939-43 covers only a portion of this war. Presumably in 1944 the large share in national product of war output, the relatively small share of the nonwar sector, particularly of nonwar capital formation, the shifts in industrial composition, in the apportionment by type of payment, in the distribution by size have at least been maintained, if they have not become more pronounced; and the same is likely to be true of the remaining years of conflict, at least until the end of the war in Europe. This means that after World War II the cumulative effects of the war shifts on postwar prospects are likely to exceed those after World War I even more than the above analysis suggests.

Appendix III

Estimates of National Product, 1914-1921

To avoid burdening the text with tables showing how the basic figures and their components were obtained, we prepared this Appendix. Assembled for reference use, the tables do not call for extensive discussion. The notes, which follow the order of the tables, are designed to be merely brief introductions.

While the analysis in Part III covers the years of World War I proper, i.e., 1914-18, most of the tables in Appendix III continue the estimates through 1919, some through 1921, to facilitate combining them with other series published by the National Bureau. The latter usually include imputed rents and net savings of governments, which are excluded here. In addition, the estimates below are based on King's estimates of income payments, which, though adjusted for some sources of noncomparability, differ somewhat from the recently estimated totals for years beginning with 1919, which are based upon more recent and extensive data.

APPENDIX TABLES III 1-3

For World War I gross national product, as defined here, can be measured by the payment-savings approach alone, i.e., as the sum of aggregate income payments, business savings of corporations and individuals, depreciation and depletion, and additions to corporate income and profits taxes. Of the adjustments necessary to render this unadjusted gross national product total comparable with the one for recent years, the most important is that for inventory revaluation. In view of the marked rise in commodity prices during World War I, business savings must have been inflated, because inventories are valued at cost or market, whichever is lower. Consequently, it seemed indispensable to adjust for the effects of this practice upon national product, approximate though the adjustment (App. Table III 1, line 8) is.

While depreciation and depletion is not large relative to other components of gross national product, its computation is statistically difficult; and for government, capital depreciation must rest upon rather crude assumptions. The main function of Appendix Table III 2 is to explain for technical students the methods of making the estimate in Appendix Table III 1.

Since the payment-savings approach is the sole method of measuring gross national product in World War I, we compare its results for recent years with the totals discussed in the text. The unadjusted gross national product for recent years in Appendix Table III 3, line 6, is comparable with that in Appendix Table III 1, line 7. It differs in merely minor respects from the gross national product total for recent years discussed in the text (line 9), and the total for World War I comparable to the latter is even closer. The one discrepancy of any size—for 1943—is less than 3 per cent.

The agreement of gross national product totals for recent years estimated by the payment-savings and final-products methods does not, of course, mean that the former yields an accurate total for World War I. All that Appendix Table III 3 proves is that no specific error need be attributed to the payment-savings approach. The estimates of income payments, business savings, depreciation and depletion for World War I are still subject to qualification.

For 1919-21 the crude estimates of gross national product, war-

APPENDIX TABLE III 1

Gross National Product, Wartime Concept, Current Prices, 1914-1921
(billions of dollars)

		1914	1915	1916	1917	1918	1919	1920	1921
1	Aggregate income payments	32.5	33.6	38.7	44.8	51.9	57.3	64.3	56.6
2	Entrepreneurial savings	0.6	1.7	3.3	6.2	4.9	7.4	2.4	—1.8
3	Corporate savings	0.2	1.4	3.0	3.6	1.2	3.6	1.4	—2.8
4	Total business savings (2 + 3)	0.8	3.1	6.4	9.8	6.0	11.0	3.8	—4.6
5	Depreciation & depletion	3.0	3.1	3.4	3.8	4.3	4.8	5.1	5.0
6	Additions to corporate income & profits taxes	0	0	0.1	2.1	3.1	2.1	1.6	0.7
7	Gross national product, unadj. (1 + 4 + 5 + 6)	36.3	39.8	48.6	60.5	65.3	75.2	74.8	57.7
8	Crude adj. for inventory revaluation	0	0	3.0	3.0	1.0	2.0	—4.0	—6.4
9	Gross national product, adj. (7 — 8)	36.3	39.8	45.6	57.5	64.3	73.2	78.8	64.1
10	War output	0.3	0.3	0.5	6.1	16.5	9.7	2.0	1.3
11	Nonwar sector (9 — 10)	36.0	39.5	45.1	51.4	47.8	63.5	76.8	62.8

LINE

1, 2, W. I. King's estimates revised (App. Table III 9) to make them comparable with Department
& 3 of Commerce estimates for recent years.

5 App. Table III 2. Excludes depreciation on owner-occupied dwellings.

6 *Statistics of Income, 1926*, p. 44.

8 The 1914-18 estimates are computed by multiplying the price changes 1914-18 by a crude ratio of inventory adjustments to price changes 1919-43, the latter measured from October to September, allowing total inventories in 1914-18 to be somewhat over one-half those for recent years (in comparable prices). For 1919-21 see Kuznets, *National Income and Its Composition*, Table VII, pp. 903 ff.

10 App. Table III 7, col. 6.

time concept, in Appendix Table III 1 can be compared with those based on more detailed recent data, prepared for a prospective monograph entitled *National Product since 1869.* These estimates, for 1919-43, linked with the detailed work underlying *National Income and Its Composition* and *Commodity Flow and Capital Formation,* can be used to check the estimates in Appendix Table III 1, once the latter have been adjusted for the difference in their

APPENDIX TABLE III 2

Depreciation and Depletion, 1913-1921

(millions of dollars)

	1913	1914	1915	1916	1917	1918	1919	1920	1921
1 Business depreciation & depletion	2,253	2,324	2,413	2,613	2,991	3,454	3,906	4,208	4,040
2 Provision for fire losses	90	90	81	122	155	208	209	218	217
3 Gov. capital depreciation	183	194	206	219	233	248	264	276	292
4 Depreciation on dwellings									
a) Total	783	812	839	867	894	905	928	977	948
b) Owner-occupied	413	430	445	462	479	487	501	534	508
c) Rented (a — b)	370	382	394	405	415	418	427	443	440
5 Total depreciation & depletion (1 + 2 + 3 + 4c)	2,896	2,990	3,094	3,359	3,794	4,328	4,806	5,145	4,989

LINE

1   Entries for 1919-21 (Solomon Fabricant, *Capital Consumption and Adjustment,* Table 29, p. 160) extrapolated for the years back to 1913 by a series of depreciation charges based on the output of capital goods (*ibid.,* Table 34, p. 182) and computed for the years back to 1913 by the method used to obtain the estimates in *ibid.* for 1919-35.

2   Entries for 1919-21 (*ibid.,* Table 4, p. 40). Computed for the years back to 1913 by the method used to obtain the estimates in *ibid.* for 1919-35.

3   Entries for 1919-21 (*ibid.,* Table 29, p. 160) extrapolated for the years back to 1913 on the basis of the rate of increase in government depreciation for 1919-35. It was not feasible to estimate the value of government capital by subtracting the annual value of new government construction because the latter was affected too much in 1917, 1918, and 1919 by inflated prices and war construction (which must have been heavily discounted in the estimates of government capital for the postwar years).

4a Entries for 1919-21 (*ibid.,* Table 29, p. 160) extrapolated for the years back to 1913 by a series for nonfarm dwellings, computed by the method used to obtain the estimates in *ibid.,* Table 25, p. 143, for 1919-35.

4b Entries for 1919-21 (*ibid.,* Table 27, p. 147). For earlier years based on ratios of owner-occupied to total dwellings— 0.736 for farm and a ratio ranging from 0.449 to 0.466 for nonfarm. For the use and sources of these ratios, see *ibid.,* pp. 143-5.

coverage. The comparison is as follows (dollar totals in billions, current prices):

		1919	1920	1921
1	Gross national product, wartime concept (App. Table III 1)	73.2	78.8	64.1
2	Imputed rent	1.5	1.9	2.2
3	Net savings of government	—1.3	1.9	1.0
4	Adj. of depreciation & depletion to reproduction value basis	—1.4	—1.8	—0.8
5	Gross national product, App. Table III 1, adj. (1 + 2 + 3 + 4)	72.0	80.8	66.5
6	Gross national product, wartime concept (*National Product since 1869*)	74.2	85.6	67.7
7	Difference between lines 5 & 6 as % of line 6	—3.0	—5.6	—1.8

Appendix Table III 3

Gross National Product, Wartime Concept
Estimated by Payments-Savings Approach, 1939-1943
(for comparison with Appendix Table III 1 and Table III 1)
(billions of dollars, current prices)

		1939	1940	1941	1942	1943
1	Income payments, incl. entrep. savings	70.8	76.2	92.7	116.6	142.3
2	Corporate savings	1.9	3.4	6.1	6.3	6.5
3	Depreciation & depletion	7.2	7.4	8.2	9.5	11.0
4	Additions to corporate income & profits taxes	0	0.3	1.6	6.0	11.2
5	Net business tax accruals, federal	0.3	1.3	4.7	4.4	2.5
6	Total, comparable to App. Table III 1, line 7 (1 + 2 + 3 + 4 + 5)	80.2	88.6	113.3	142.8	173.5
7	Adj. for inventory revaluation	—0.4	—0.4	—3.2	—2.1	—0.2
8	Total, comparable to App. Table III 1, line 9 and Table III 1, line 4 (6 + 7)	79.8	88.2	110.1	140.7	173.3
9	Total used in Table III 1, line 4	79.4	88.3	111.4	144.2	178.1
	Further adjustments in reconciling lines 8 and 9					
10	Excess of contributions to social insurance over transfer payments	—0.4	—0.5	+0.1	+0.5	+0.6
11	Net business tax accruals, state & local	0	0	0.1	0.1	0.1
12	Statistical discrepancies (Dept. of Commerce adj.)	0	—0.4	—1.7	—0.6	1.2
13	Adj. total, comparable to line 9 (8 + 10 + 11 + 12)	79.4	87.3	108.6	140.7	175.2

LINE

1 *Survey of Current Business,* April 1944, p. 14, Table 12, line 5.

2 Adjusted for additions to 'other' business reserves and capital outlay charged to current expense; *ibid.,* p. 13, Table 11, line 11, and p. 14, Table 13, lines 4 and 5.

3 Table II 1, lines 2a — 2b + 3a — 3b.

4 *Survey,* April 1944, p. 10, Table B, line 2.

5 *Ibid.,* line 17.

7 *Ibid.,* p. 14, Table 13, line 6.

10 *Ibid.,* p. 13, Table 12, lines 2 and 4.

LINE

11 *Ibid.,* p. 10, Table B, line 38.

12 *Ibid.,* p. 14, Table 13, line 7.

The differences are not of an order to render the estimates in Appendix Table III 1 invalid for approximate analysis. Even if we consider that they apply to the nonwar sector alone, war output being identical in the two series, they do not exceed in 1920, the year of the biggest discrepancy, 6 per cent of the total derived with the more extensive recent data.

Appendix Tables III 4-5

The various series used to adjust gross national product and its components for price changes are assembled in Appendix Table III 4. The footnotes give the weights assigned in constructing group indexes for the three components of gross national product: flow of goods to consumers, capital goods entering nonwar capital formation, and war output. The weights are approximate, since there is no information by which gross national product in current prices can be allocated precisely to the categories for which a differential price adjustment is justified.

According to the over-all price indexes implicit in gross national product (Table III 1), prices moved more or less similarly during the first four years of each war (1914-17 and 1939-42), and diverged widely only in the fifth year (1918 and 1943). The composite index of earnings, which covers the majority of persons employed, offers confirming evidence (App. Table III 5).

Appendix Table III 6

The first three lines in Appendix Table III 6 are derived from Appendix Tables III 1 and 4. The contribution of Appendix Table III 6 is in lines 4-11—an independent estimate of the flow of goods to consumers 1914-18.

This estimate is based, in general, upon the flow of finished products at producers' current prices, converted to 1914 prices, adjusted to final cost to consumers, and corrected for changes in finished inventories. Since data for these early years with which each successive step could be estimated precisely are scarce, line 11 cannot be anything except an approximation. The year-to-year changes are especially vulnerable. Yet line 11 checks pretty well with line 1. In every year flow of goods to consumers is less than nonwar output, as it should be, since the latter includes gross nonwar capital formation. It is also reasonable that gross nonwar capital formation, derived from lines 1 and 11, is fairly high during 1914-17, lowest in

APPENDIX TABLE III 4

Price Indexes Used to Adjust Gross National Product
for Price Changes, 1914-1921
(1914 = 100)

Price Indexes for:	1914	1915	1916	1917	1918	1919	1920	1921
1 Consumer goods	100.0	100.5	108.2	126.2	148.9	171.6	194.8	170.7
2 Capital goods								
a) Construction costs	100.0	103.0	117.2	146.3	167.9	192.5	238.8	190.3
b) Producer durable	100.0	106.1	120.1	145.1	175.2	183.5	180.5	164.0
c) Total (av. of a & b)	100.0	104.6	118.6	145.7	171.6	188.0	209.6	177.2
3 Total nonwar	100.0	101.5	110.3	129.8	149.8	174.0	196.9	171.1
4 Total war								
a) Pay	100.0	100.0	100.0	100.0	100.0	100.0	100.0	100.0
b) Subsistence, clothing								
& other soft items	100.0	101.2	120.4	162.8	197.0	210.4	242.8	162.3
c) Producer durable	100.0	106.1	120.1	145.1	175.2	183.5	180.5	164.0
d) Construction costs	100.0	103.0	117.2	146.3	167.9	192.5	238.8	190.3
e) Total	100.0	103.3	115.6	148.2	170.2	181.5	179.4	147.2
5 Gross national product								
(implicit)	100.0	101.5	110.4	131.6	154.6	175.1	196.5	170.5

LINE

1   Calculated from W. I. King, *National Income and Its Purchasing Power*, Tables VIII and IX, pp. 74 and 77.

2a   Solomon Fabricant, *Capital Consumption and Adjustment*, Table 32, p. 178.

2b   W. H. Shaw, 'Finished Commodities since 1879', National Bureau *Occasional Paper 3*, Aug. 1941, Table 1, p. 7.

3   Index implicit in nonwar goods. Value of consumer goods, in current prices, is from data underlying Appendix Table III 6, line 11 and comparable figures for 1919-21; value of nonwar capital goods in current prices obtained by subtraction. Lines 1 and 2c were used to convert to 1914 prices.

4a   Assumed constant.

4b   Simple average of price indexes for consumer perishable and semidurable commodities (see W. H. Shaw, *op. cit.*, Table 1).

4c   Identical with 2b.

4d   Identical with 2a.

4e   Weighted average of (a)-(d). The weights, annual expenditures, were computed by allocating war expenditures to durable and nondurable groups. Nondurable was divided into pay and other by using figures on pay from unpublished National Bureau data. Durable was divided into producer durable and construction by using Chawner's data on military construction (*Construction Activity in the United States*, Washington, D.C., 1938).

5   Line 9 of App. Table III 1 divided by line 3 of App. Table III 6.

the depression year 1914, and declines markedly in 1918. As the estimates in lines 1 and 11 were made independently, the reasonable character of their relative levels and movements tends to support both.

APPENDIX TABLES III 7-8

These tables provide a rather detailed explanation of the quarterly interpolation of gross national product and its war and nonwar sectors, in both current and 1914 prices. In general the steps were to: (a) estimate gross national product, in current prices, quarterly;

APPENDIX TABLE III 5
Hourly Earnings Indexes, Selected Industries
World Wars I and II

WORLD WAR I (1914 = 100)

	1914	1915	1916	1917	1918
1 Manufacturing	100	100	111	127	156
2 Anthracite coal	100	112	117	155	211
3 Bituminous coal	100	104	117	150	185
4 Union building trades	100	100	104	110	121
5 Railroads	100	105	108	122	177
6 Composite index, New York FRB	100	101	109	123	151

WORLD WAR II (1939 = 100)

	1939	1940	1941	1942	1943
7 Manufacturing	100	104	115	135	152
8 Anthracite coal	100	100	105	107	116
9 Bituminous coal	100	100	111	120	129
10 Building construction	100	103	108	124	134
11 Railroads	100	100	104	114	116
12 Composite index, New York FRB	100	103	110	124	137

LINE

1-5 Paul Douglas, *Real Wages in the United States, 1890-1926* (Houghton Mifflin, 1930). Based on hourly earnings in Table 24, p. 108; Table 39, p. 135; Table 48, p. 152; Table 52, p. 161; and footnote 2, p. 167. Line 5, 1914, is based on average full-time weekly earnings, assuming a 10 hour day and a 6 day week.

6 From *Monthly Review of Credit and Business Conditions* (New York Federal
& 12 Reserve Bank). The index includes hourly earnings in various industries (farm wage rates, manufacturing, bituminous coal mining, railway, new utilities, retail trade for recent years) and weekly wages or annual salaries for office employees and teachers. The data for 1914-18 are unpublished revisions and were obtained directly from the Federal Reserve Bank.

7-10 Bureau of Labor Statistics. Average of monthly data.

11 Based on an unpublished average hourly earnings series compiled by Leo Wolman from total compensation and service hours and days (Interstate Commerce Commission, *Monthly Wage Statistics*).

Gross National Product, Wartime Concept, 1914 Prices, 1914-1921
(billions of dollars)

	1914	1915	1916	1917	1918	1919	1920	1921
1 Nonwar output	36.0	38.9	40.9	39.6	31.9	36.5	39.0	36.7
2 War output	0.3	0.3	0.4	4.1	9.7	5.3	1.1	0.9
3 Gross national product (1 + 2)	36.3	39.2	41.3	43.7	41.6	41.8	40.1	37.6

APPROXIMATION TO CONSUMERS' OUTLAY

4 Perishable commodities	12.44	11.84	12.31	12.40	12.74			
5 Semidurable commodities	4.24	3.72	4.57	4.62	4.59			
6 Durable commodities	2.51	2.84	3.81	3.95	3.42			
7 Adj. for war share	0.1	0.1	0.1	0.6	1.5			
8 Total (4 + 5 + 6 — 7)	19.1	18.3	20.6	20.4	19.3			
9 Services	11.5	11.0	12.4	12.3	11.6			
10 Consumers' outlay (8 + 9)	30.6	29.3	33.0	32.7	30.9			
11 Consumers' outlay excl. imputed rent	29.5	28.2	32.0	31.9	30.2			

LINE

1 Line 11 of App. Table III 1 divided by line 3 of App. Table III 4.

2 Line 10 of App. Table III 1 divided by line 4e of App. Table III 4.

4 Output at producers' current prices, converted to 1914 prices, adjusted to final cost to consumers, and corrected for net change in finished inventories. Output at producers' prices and the price index, with 1913 as base, are from W. H. Shaw, *Occasional Paper 3*, Table 1. The ratio of the retail value to producers' value represents the relation in 1919-33 of the retail value of output destined for domestic consumption (the value of output destined for domestic consumption at producers' prices plus transportation and distributive charges), plus the farm value of products retained by farmers for their own consumption, to the value of output destined for domestic consumption at producers' prices plus the farm value of products retained by farmers for their own consumption. Data for this ratio are from Simon Kuznets, *Commodity Flow and Capital Formation* (National Bureau of Economic Research, 1938), Tables II-7, V-7 and 8. For the net change in inventories, 1914-18, the procedure is as follows:

Dun's Review, Feb. 1940, gives sample data for 1913-22 on inventories held by manufacturers of foods, chemicals, oil, paper, and tobacco, and by meat packers. These, weighted by the value of ouput reported for 1914 and 1919 in the *Census of Manufactures*, yield annual indexes of perishable finished inventories for 1913-22, in current prices. These indexes are added for 1913-18 and for 1918-22.

To get total inventories for 1913-18, the ratio of the sum of the indexes for 1913-18 to those for 1918-22 is multiplied by the total value of perishable inventories, after mark-up, for 1918-22. Perishable inventories, before mark-up are shown annually 1918-22 in Kuznets, *op. cit.*, Table V-7, lines A3 and 7. The mark-up is calculated from 1929 data in the same table.

Inventories in 1913 are estimated by dividing total inventories for 1913-18 by the sum of the annual indexes and multiplying by 100. Annual values in current prices for 1914-18 are extrapolated from the 1913 value by the annual indexes of inventories. They are converted to 1914 prices by the price index used for output. Annual net changes are then computed.

LINE

5 The procedure is the same as for line 4. For output at producers' prices and for the price index the sources are the same. The ratio of retail to producers' value is calculated from Kuznets, *op. cit.*, Table III 5, p. 212, col. 5 and 4. For the net change in inventories, 1914-18, the procedure is as follows:

Dun's Review, Feb. 1940, gives sample data for 1913-22 on inventories held by manufacturers of rubber and by mass distributors. These, weighted by the value of output reported for 1914 and 1919 in the *Census of Manufactures,* yield annual indexes of semidurable finished inventories for 1913-22 in current prices. These indexes are added for 1913-18 and for 1918-22.

To get total inventories for 1913-18, the ratio of the sum of the indexes for 1913-18 to those for 1918-22 is multiplied by the total value of semidurable inventories, after mark-up, for 1918-22. Semidurable inventories, before mark-up, are shown annually 1918-22 in Kuznets, *op. cit.,* Table V-7, lines B3 and 7. The mark-up is calculated from 1929 data in the same table.

Inventories in 1913 are estimated by dividing total inventories for 1913-18 by the sum of the annual indexes and multiplying by 100. Annual values in current prices for 1914-18 are extrapolated from the 1913 value by the annual indexes of inventories. They are converted to 1914 prices by the price index used for output. Annual net changes are then computed.

6 The procedure is the same as for line 4. For output at producers' prices and for the price index the sources are the same. The ratio of retail to producers' value is calculated from the 1919-33 retail value of output destined for domestic consumption and the value at producers' prices. Data for this ratio are from Kuznets, *op. cit.,* Table II-7, and a revision of Table V-7 to be published in *National Product since 1869.* For the net change in inventories, 1914-18, the procedure is as follows:

Dun's Review, Feb. 1940, gives sample data for 1913-22 on inventories held by manufacturers of automobiles and of miscellaneous consumer goods. These, weighted by the value of output reported for 1914 and 1919 in the *Census of Manufactures,* yield annual indexes of consumer durable finished inventories for 1913-22, in current prices. These indexes are added for 1913-18 and for 1918-22.

To get total inventories for 1913-18, the ratio of the sum of the indexes for 1913-18 to those for 1918-22 is multiplied by the total value of consumer durable inventories, after mark-up, for 1918-22. Consumer durable inventories before mark-up, are shown annually 1918-22 in Kuznets, *op. cit.,* Table V-7, lines 5 and 9, under Consumers' Durable. The mark-up is calculated from 1929 data in the same table.

Inventories in 1913 are estimated by dividing total inventories for 1913-18 by the sum of the annual indexes and multiplying by 100. Annual values in current prices 1914-18, extrapolated from the 1913 value by the annual indexes of inventories, are converted to 1914 prices by the price index used for output. Annual net changes are then computed.

7 Line 2 x 0.15.

9 The ratio of services to consumer commodities, 1914-18, is that calculated from the values of these two items, 1869-1918, in *National Product since 1869.*

11 Difference between line 10, converted to current prices by Appendix Table III 4, line 1, and imputed rent in King, *National Income and Its Purchasing Power,* p. 379, reconverted to 1914 prices by the same index.

Appendix Table III 7

Gross National Product, Wartime Concept, Quarterly Interpolation
Current Prices, 1914-1921
(dollar figures in billions, annual rates)

	INDUSTRIAL PRODUCTION INDEX (1)	OVERALL PRICE INDEX (2)	INDUSTRIAL PRODUCTION INDEX Current prices (3)	INDEX ADJ. TO MOVEMENT OF GROSS NATIONAL PRODUCT (4)	GROSS NATIONAL PRODUCT (5)	WAR OUTPUT (6)	NONWAR OUTPUT (7)
1914			100.0	100.0	36.3	0.3	36.0
I	103	100	103	103	37.4	0.3	37.1
II	102	99	101	101	36.7	0.3	36.4
III	100	101	101	101	36.7	0.4	36.3
IV	95	100	95	95	34.5	0.3	34.2
1915			109.8	109.6	39.8	0.3	39.5
I	102	100	102	102	37.0	0.3	36.7
II	106	100	106	106	38.5	0.3	38.2
III	110	101	111	111	40.3	0.4	39.9
IV	114	105	120	120	43.6	0.3	43.3
1916			125.2	125.6	45.6	0.5	45.1
I	118	108	127	126	45.7	0.3	45.4
II	114	109	124	124	45.0	0.3	44.7
III	110	110	121	121	43.9	0.7	43.2
IV	113	114	129	130	47.2	0.5	46.7
1917			159.2	158.4	57.5	6.1	51.4
I	117	120	140	140	50.8	0.5	50.3
II	123	130	160	159	57.7	4.6	53.1
III	120	137	164	163	59.2	8.2	51.0
IV	122	142	173	171	62.1	11.2	50.9
1918			178.5	177.1	64.3	16.5	47.8
I	114	146	166	166	60.3	11.9	48.4
II	116	154	179	178	64.6	15.5	49.1
III	117	159	186	185	67.2	18.0	49.2
IV	113	162	183	181	65.7	20.6	45.1
1919			202.8	201.7	73.2	9.7	63.5
I	113	159	180	179	65.0	15.8	49.2
II	112	161	180	179	65.0	11.7	53.3
III	119	186	221	220	79.9	7.8	72.1
IV	117	197	230	229	83.1	3.4	79.7
1920			217.0	217.1	78.8	2.0	76.8
I	117	201	235	235	85.3	2.2	83.1
II	112	204	228	228	82.8	2.4	80.4
III	108	201	217	217	78.8	2.0	76.8
IV	105	179	188	188	68.2	1.5	66.7
1921			176.2	176.6	64.1	1.3	62.8
I	102	175	178	178	64.6	1.6	63.0
II	102	170	173	174	63.2	1.4	61.8
III	104	168	175	175	63.5	1.0	62.5
IV	106	169	179	179	65.0	1.1	63.9

COLUMN

1 Federal Reserve Board index of production (*Federal Reserve Bulletin,* May 1924, p. 422), corrected for seasonal variations, was first adjusted to the annual movements of gross national product in constant prices (see App. Table III 6). Then intra-annual fluctuations were reduced to one-half their original amplitude to allow for the smaller sensitivity of the gross national product totals.

2 Based upon a combination of Bureau of Labor Statistics group indexes of wholesale prices. For nonwar output the following group indexes were combined, weighted as indicated: food, 3.5; fuel and lighting, 1.0; chemicals and drugs, 1.0; textile products, 2.0; hides and leather products, 0.5; house furnishing goods, 1.0; miscellaneous, 1.0; metal products, 1.0; building materials, 1.0. The weights for metal products and building materials were reduced to total 1.5 in 1917 and 1.0 in 1918. This index of prices for nonwar output was then adjusted to the annual levels in Appendix Table III 4.

The index of prices for war output utilized the following monthly BLS group indexes: (1) Combination of food, fuel and lighting; chemicals and drugs; textiles; and hides and leather—with the internal weights proportionate to the ones used for nonwar output. This combined index was given the weight of 1.5; (2) metal products, 6.0; (3) building materials, 1.5. These three indexes were then combined with an index kept at 100 (weight 1.0) to yield a preliminary quarterly index of prices for war output, which was then adjusted to the annual totals in Appendix Table III 4.

The two indexes for nonwar output and for war output described in the two preceding paragraphs were combined by being weighted in accordance with the percentage distribution of gross national product in current prices (App. Table III 1).

3 (Col. 1 x col. 2) ÷ 100.

4 The adjustment to the annual levels of gross national product in current prices in Appendix Table III 1 was minor; indeed, perceptible in 1917 and 1918 alone.

5 Col. 4 x $36.3 billion (gross national product in 1914).

6 Quarterly estimates based on fiscal year data in the *Annual Report of the Secretary of the Treasury.* For 1914-16 the data include the War and Navy Departments; in 1917 the U. S. Shipping Board, Food and Fuel Administration, and foreign loans are added; in 1918 the War Finance Corporation and federal control of transportation are added; in 1919 the Food and Fuel Administration is dropped and the Grain Corporation is added. For 1914-16 the fiscal year totals are divided into quarters by means of partial quarterly figures from *ibid.* For fiscal years 1917-19 the breakdown is based on quarterly figures for total ordinary expenditures, except foreign loans, which are reported monthly; for 1919-22 the quarterly estimates are based on the monthly figures reported in the daily Treasury statement.

The final series is reduced by the major items of receipts on war account reported in *ibid.,* including interest on foreign obligations, principal payments on foreign obligations, sale of Army and Navy war supplies, and decrease in capital stock of the U. S. Grain Corporation. These data are reported solely by fiscal years; calendar year estimates are averages of fiscal year totals. War output, net of these receipts, is distributed by quarters on the assumption that its distribution is the same as that of total war ouput.

7 Col. 5 — col. 6.

APPENDIX TABLE III 8

Gross National Product, Wartime Concept, Quarterly Interpolation
1914 Prices, 1914-1921
(dollar figures in billions, annual rates)

	NONWAR OUTPUT			WAR OUTPUT			GROSS NATIONAL PRODUCT	
	Totals, current prices	Price index (1914=100)	Totals, 1914 prices	Totals, current prices	Price index (1914=100)	Totals, 1914 prices	Totals, 1914 prices	Implicit price index (1914=100)
	(1)	(2)	(3)	(4)	(5)	(6)	(7)	(8)
1914	36.0	100	36.0	0.3	100.0	0.3	36.3	100.0
I	37.1	100	37.1	0.3	102	0.3	37.4	100.0
II	36.4	99	36.8	0.3	100	0.3	37.1	98.9
III	36.3	101	35.9	0.4	100	0.4	36.3	101.1
IV	34.2	100	34.2	0.3	98	0.3	34.5	100.0
1915	39.5	101.5	38.9	0.3	101.5	0.3	39.2	101.5
I	36.7	100	36.7	0.3	99	0.3	37.0	100.0
II	38.2	100	38.2	0.3	101	0.3	38.5	100.0
III	39.9	101	39.5	0.4	102	0.4	39.9	101.0
IV	43.3	105	41.2	0.3	104	0.3	41.5	105.1
1916	45.1	110.3	40.9	0.5	115.6	0.4	41.3	110.4
I	45.4	108	42.0	0.3	110	0.3	42.3	108.0
II	44.7	109	41.0	0.3	116	0.3	41.3	109.0
III	43.2	110	39.3	0.7	115	0.6	39.9	110.0
IV	46.7	114	41.0	0.5	122	0.4	41.4	114.0
1917	51.4	129.8	39.6	6.1	148.2	4.1	43.7	131.6
I	50.3	120	41.9	0.5	133	0.4	42.3	120.1
II	53.1	128	41.5	4.6	145	3.2	44.7	129.1
III	51.0	134	38.1	8.2	155	5.3	43.4	136.4
IV	50.9	137	37.2	11.2	160	7.0	44.2	140.5
1918	47.8	149.8	31.9	16.5	170.2	9.7	41.6	154.6
I	48.4	141	34.3	11.9	161	7.4	41.7	144.6
II	49.1	149	33.0	15.5	167	9.3	42.3	152.7
III	49.2	153	32.2	18.0	175	10.3	42.5	158.1
IV	45.1	156	28.9	20.6	178	11.6	40.5	162.2
1919	63.5	174.0	36.5	9.7	181.5	5.3	41.8	175.1
I	49.2	154	31.9	15.8	176	9.0	40.9	158.9
II	53.3	159	33.5	11.7	175	6.7	40.2	161.7
III	72.1	186	38.8	7.8	184	4.2	43.0	185.8
IV	79.7	197	40.5	3.4	191	1.8	42.3	196.5
1920	76.8	196.9	39.0	2.0	179.4	1.1	40.1	196.5
I	83.1	201	41.3	2.2	193	1.1	42.4	201.2
II	80.4	205	39.2	2.4	187	1.3	40.5	204.4
III	76.8	202	38.0	2.0	175	1.1	39.1	201.5
IV	66.7	180	37.1	1.5	163	0.9	38.0	179.5
1921	62.8	171.1	36.7	1.3	147.2	0.9	37.6	170.5
I	63.0	176	35.8	1.6	155	1.0	36.8	175.5
II	61.8	171	36.1	1.4	149	0.9	37.0	170.8
III	62.5	168	37.2	1.0	144	0.7	37.9	167.5
IV	63.9	170	37.6	1.1	141	0.8	38.4	169.3

COLUMN
1 App. Table III 7, col. 7.
2 See App. Table III 7, notes to col. 2.
3 (Col. 1 ÷ col. 2)100.
4 App. Table III 7, col. 6.

COLUMN
5 See App. Table III 7, notes to col. 2.
6 (Col. 4 ÷ col. 5)100.
7 Col. 3 + col. 6.
8 (Col. 5 of App. Table III 7 ÷ col. 7)100.

(b) subtract from (a) quarterly data on war output, in current prices, thereby deriving quarterly estimates in current prices for the nonwar sector; (c) compute quarterly indexes of prices, separately for the war and nonwar sectors; (d) adjust the quarterly totals under (b) for price changes. The annual totals, in both current and 1914 prices, are controlling throughout. The quarterly interpolations, based on monthly indexes of much narrower scope, are naturally less reliable. But it seemed worth while to calculate them in order to approximate more specific periods in the comparison of the two wars.

APPENDIX TABLE III 9

This table presents in detail the industry-type-of-income components for 1914-21. While based upon W. I. King's work, they are adjusted to attain closer comparability with the estimates for recent years.

APPENDIX TABLE III 9
Income Payments-Net Business Savings Aggregate
Current Prices, 1914-1921
(millions of dollars)

	1914	1915	1916	1917	1918	1919	1920	1921
AGRICULTURE								
1 Wages & salaries	756	773	828	1,030	1,213	1,491	1,663	1,405
2 Entrepreneurial withdrawals	3,154	3,185	3,482	4,307	5,034	6,036	6,907	5,872
3 Entrepreneurial savings	237	567	1,275	2,679	3,658	3,151	898	—1,870
4 Interest	101	110	125	144	160	200	238	247
5 Net income	4,248	4,635	5,710	8,160	10,065	10,878	9,706	5,654
MINING								
1 Wages & salaries	695	701	881	1,105	1,376	1,416	1,848	1,414
2 Entrepreneurial withdrawals	14	14	29	34	28	16	12	16
3 Entrepreneurial savings	1	12	15	4	—4	8	25	—19
4 Dividends	151	143	371	429	359	207	149	183
5 Interest	23	25	27	29	32	36	41	47
6 Corporate savings	10	150	195	51	—54	—13	147	—449
7 Net income	894	1,045	1,518	1,652	1,737	1,670	2,222	1,192
MANUFACTURING								
1 Wages & salaries	4,791	5,117	6,751	8,491	10,640	11,862	14,255	9,589
2 Other employee compensation	72	83	189	135	166	161	238	143
3 Total employee compensation	4,863	5,200	6,940	8,626	10,806	12,023	14,493	9,732
4 Entrepreneurial withdrawals	259	257	384	409	359	324	301	253
5 Entrepreneurial savings	15	157	362	354	91	437	49	—184
6 Dividends	890	945	1,695	1,957	1,861	1,786	1,728	1,549
7 Interest	178	182	186	191	197	206	218	227
8 Corporate savings	66	762	1,888	1,992	561	2,305	914	—1,760
9 Net income	6,271	7,503	11,455	13,529	13,875	17,081	17,703	9,817

Appendix Table III 9 continued:

	1914	1915	1916	1917	1918	1919	1920	1921
			CONSTRUCTION					
1 Wages & salaries	876	874	968	938	1,003	1,451	1,447	1,316
2 Entrep. withdrawals, div., & int.	536	520	548	268	204	395	448	424
3 Entrepreneurial savings	30	128	225	135	36	181	77	—27
4 Corporate savings	8	34	68	36	9	22	12	—28
5 Net income	1,450	1,556	1,809	1,377	1,252	2,049	1,984	1,685
		STEAM RAILROADS, PULLMAN, AND EXPRESS						
1 Wages & salaries	1,425	1,435	1,607	1,907	2,842	3,107	4,045	3,062
2 Other employee compensation	28	29	33	36	40	46	58	43
3 Total employee compensation	1,453	1,464	1,640	1,943	2,882	3,153	4,103	3,105
4 Miscellaneous railroad income	8	8	8	9	9	10	16	10
5 Dividends	281	255	260	274	259	256	236	208
6 Interest	399	437	437	440	433	436	462	477
7 Corporate savings	—42	83	241	185	22	58	—6	—5
8 Net income	2,099	2,247	2,586	2,851	3,605	3,913	4,811	3,795
			STREET RAILWAYS					
1 Wages & salaries	222	225	243	267	312	376	478	472
2 Dividends	72	70	74	68	56	53	51	49
3 Interest	115	119	121	119	119	124	122	125
4 Corporate savings	15	9	16	9	—5	12	22	28
5 Net income	424	423	454	463	482	565	673	674
			WATER TRANSPORTATION					
1 Wages & salaries	203	223	274	333	417	590	809	666
2 Entrepreneurial withdrawals	7	8	9	21	20	26	18	14
3 Entrepreneurial savings	—	11	32	8	15	8	5	—2
4 Dividends	18	18	24	51	43	64	45	33
5 Interest	24	27	32	31	24	30	24	27
6 Corporate savings	—1	26	73	19	31	22	19	—24
7 Net income	251	313	444	463	550	740	920	714
			TELEPHONE					
1 Wages & salaries	128	126	146	170	190	242	319	330
2 Other employee compensation	1	2	8	3	4	4	4	4
3 Total employee compensation	129	128	154	173	194	246	323	334
4 Uncollectible revenue	1	1	2	2	2	2	3	3
5 Dividends	31	33	36	39	40	40	41	46
6 Interest	22	22	23	25	27	31	37	42
7 Corporate savings	13	19	27	17	15	14	9	23
8 Net income	196	203	242	256	278	333	413	448
			TELEGRAPH					
1 Wages & salaries	27	25	35	44	59	67	93	80
2 Other employee compensation	—	1	1	1	1	2	1	2
3 Total employee compensation	27	26	36	45	60	69	94	82
4 Dividends	10	11	11	13	14	14	14	13
5 Interest	2	2	2	1	2	2	2	2
6 Corporate savings	—3	2	3	4	6	11	12	8
7 Net income	36	41	52	63	82	96	122	105
		ELECTRIC LIGHT & POWER & MFD. GAS						
1 Wages & salaries	110	117	130	143	160	196	243	258
2 Dividends	44	49	54	60	67	73	80	93
3 Interest	42	46	50	57	70	75	83	93
4 Corporate savings	19	22	29	30	28	36	45	45
5 Net income	215	234	263	290	325	380	451	489

		1914	1915	1916	1917	1918	1919	1920	1921
				TRADE					
1	Wages & salaries	2,087	2,155	2,370	2,647	2,963	3,482	4,116	3,853
2	Entrepreneurial withdrawals	1,980	1,993	2,176	2,847	2,902	3,483	3,412	2,898
3	Entrepreneurial savings	121	154	268	1,203	450	2,426	419	—458
4	Dividends	193	163	211	247	322	359	371	393
5	Interest	113	126	141	156	172	192	209	216
6	Corporate savings	77	100	177	809	310	624	8	—462
7	Net income	4,571	4,691	5,343	7,909	7,119	10,566	8,535	6,440
				BANKING					
1	Wages & salaries	164	183	214	230	281	362	429	481
2	Dividends	111	99	81	81	87	67	108	148
3	Corporate savings	61	69	124	153	194	210	187	100
4	Net income	336	351	419	464	562	639	724	729
				GOVERNMENT					
1	Wages & salaries	1,656	1,734	1,821	2,464	5,272	4,489	3,519	3,751
2	Other employee compensation	205	202	204	219	469	583	713	813
3	Total employee compensation	1,861	1,936	2,025	2,683	5,741	5,072	4,232	4,564
4	Interest	232	257	272	361	537	1,064	1,078	1,065
5	Net income	2,093	2,193	2,297	3,044	6,278	6,136	5,310	5,629
				UNCLASSIFIED					
1	Wages & salaries	4,789	5,047	5,343	5,096	4,219	4,677	5,749	6,082
2	Entrep. withdrawals, div., & int.	2,400	2,436	2,510	3,302	3,037	3,026	3,073	3,076
3	Entrepreneurial savings	147	665	1,136	1,832	618	1,237	954	809
4	Div. & int., international	—85	—68	—46	—51	—26	—17	—8	—7
5	Corporate savings	23	95	207	271	53	279	—9	—287
6	Net income	7,274	8,175	9,150	10,450	7,901	9,202	9,759	9,673
				RENT PAID					
1	Total rent paid	2,979	3,104	3,322	3,592	3,819	4,122	4,738	4,962
		INCOME PAYMENTS-BUSINESS SAVINGS AGGREGATE							
1	Wages & salaries	17,929	18,735	21,611	24,865	30,947	33,808	39,013	32,759
2	Other employee compensation	306	317	435	394	680	796	1,014	1,005
3	Total employee compensation	18,235	19,052	22,046	25,259	31,627	34,604	40,027	33,764
4	Entrepreneurial withdrawals	7,892	7,912	8,414	10,438	10,965	12,822	13,714	12,138
5	Entrepreneurial savings	551	1,694	3,313	6,215	4,864	7,448	2,427	—1,751
6	Dividends	2,055	2,074	3,336	3,774	3,544	3,226	3,111	2,958
7	Interest	1,464	1,575	1,631	1,760	1,967	2,585	2,702	2,753
8	Div. & int., international	—85	—68	—46	—51	—26	—17	—8	—7
9	Rent	2,979	3,104	3,322	3,592	3,819	4,122	4,738	4,962
10	Corporate savings	246	1,371	3,048	3,576	1,170	3,580	1,360	—2,811
11	Income payments-business savings aggregate	33,337	36,714	45,064	54,563	57,930	68,370	68,071	52,006

LINE AGRICULTURE

1 W. I. King, *National Income and Its Purchasing Power*, p. 122.

2 Difference between entrepreneurial net income (*ibid.*, p. 308) and line 3.

3 Simon Kuznets, *National Income and Its Composition*, pp. 470 and 456.

4 King, *op. cit.*, p. 308.

5 Sum of lines 1 through 4.

MINING

1 King, *op. cit.*, p. 122.

2 Difference between realized income of entrepreneurs and property holders (*ibid.*, p. 108) and dividends and interest (see note to lines 4 and 5) and rent (unpublished worksheets underlying the estimates).

Appendix Table III 9 continued:

LINE   MINING *(concl.)*

3 *1914-18:* difference between total and corporate savings (for the latter see notes to line 6).
Total savings are obtained by raising corporate by the ratio of the total value of product to corporate (*Census of Mines and Quarries* for 1909 and 1919) and interpolating along a straight
line for the intercensal years.

1919-21: Kuznets, *op. cit.,* p. 312.

4 & 5 King, *op. cit.,* pp. 186, 189, 191.

6 *1914-18:* difference between corporate net income after taxes (*Statistics of Income for 1916-18*
and extrapolated back to 1914 by a corporate sample) and dividends paid. For 1918 net dividends (see note to line 4) are subtracted since the net income figures exclude dividend receipts
by corporations; for the earlier years, gross dividends are subtracted (King, *op. cit.,* pp. 182
and 184).

1919-21: Kuznets, *op. cit.,* p. 312.

7 Sum of lines 1 through 6.

MANUFACTURING

1 Difference between wages and salaries (King, *op. cit.,* pp. 132, 138) and 'duplication' and
'transfer to other industries' (Kuznets, *op. cit.,* pp. 470 and 456).

2 Difference between total employee compensation and wages and salaries (King, *op. cit.,* pp.
122, 132, 138).

3 Sum of lines 1 and 2.

4 See notes to *Mining,* line 2.

5 See notes to *Mining,* line 3. The ratio of the total value of product to corporate is from unpublished worksheets underlying the estimates in King, *op. cit.*

6 & 7 See notes to *Mining,* lines 4 and 5.

8 See notes to *Mining,* line 6.

9 Sum of lines 3 through 8.

CONSTRUCTION

1 See notes to *Mining,* line 1.

2 King, *op. cit.,* p. 108.

3 *1914-18:* total savings estimated by applying to line 2 the ratio of savings to entrepreneurial
& withdrawals, dividends, and interest computed from the totals for mining, manufacturing, steam
4 railroads, street railways, water transportation, telephone, telegraph, electric light and power,
trade, and banking. The division into entrepreneurial and corporate savings for 1917 and 1918
is based on unpublished estimates by W. I. King for profits of individual contractors and corporate contractors; for 1914-16, the ratio of individual savings to total is extrapolated by the
similar ratio for the unclassified industries.

5 Sum of lines 1 through 4.

1919-21: Kuznets, *op. cit.,* p. 312.

STEAM RAILROADS, PULLMAN, AND EXPRESS

1 King, *op. cit.,* pp. 133, 139.

2 Difference between lines 1 and 3.

3 King, *op. cit.,* p. 123.

4 Unpublished estimates of uncollectible revenue and compensation for injuries to nonemployees.

5 & 6 King, *op. cit.,* pp. 186, 189, 191.

7 *1914-18:* computed from data in *Statistics of Railways and Preliminary Abstract of Statistics of
Common Carriers* (Interstate Commerce Commission).

1919-21: Kuznets, *op. cit.,* p. 673.

8 Sum of lines 3 through 7.

LINE
STREET RAILWAYS
1-3 King, *op. cit.*, pp. 123, 186, 189, 191.

4 *1917 and 1918:* see notes describing estimates for 1919 and later years in Kuznets, *op. cit.*, Part Four; 1914-16 savings are estimated by interpolating between the 1912 and 1917 Census values by a corporate sample.
1919-21: ibid., p. 674.

5 Sum of lines 1 through 4.

WATER TRANSPORTATION
1 King, *op. cit.*, p. 123.

2 & 4 Unpublished data underlying the estimates in *ibid.*

3 & 6 *1914-18:* see notes to lines 2 and 4.
1919-21: Kuznets, *op. cit.*, pp. 662 and 674.

5 *Ibid.*, p. 186.

7 Sum of lines 1 through 6.

TELEPHONE
1 King, *op. cit.*, pp. 133, 139.

2 Difference between lines 1 and 3.

3 King, *op. cit.*, p. 123.

4 Unpublished data underlying the estimates in *ibid.*

5 & 6 See *ibid.*, pp. 186, 189, 191.

7 See notes to *Street Railways*, line 4.

8 Sum of lines 3 through 7.

TELEGRAPH
1 King, *op. cit.*, pp. 133, 139.

2 Difference between lines 1 and 3.

3 King, *op. cit.*, p. 123.

4 & 5 *Ibid.*, pp. 186, 189, 191.

6 *1917 and 1918:* see notes describing estimates for 1919 and later years in Kuznets, *op. cit.*, Part Four; 1914-16 savings are the difference between net income and gross dividends paid. Net income (for 1912 and 1917 from the *Census of Electrical Industries*) is interpolated for intercensal years by the net income of Western Union Telegraph Company reported in the *Statistical Abstract*. Gross dividends are from King, *op. cit.*, pp. 182 and 184.
1919-21: Kuznets, *op. cit.*, p. 674.

7 Sum of lines 3 through 6.

ELECTRIC LIGHT AND POWER AND MANUFACTURED GAS
1 Sum of wages and salaries in electric light and power (King, *op. cit.*, p. 123) and in manufactured gas (*Census of Manufactures* for 1914 and 1919, interpolated for 1915-18 with the estimates for electric light and power as index). For 1920 and 1921, Kuznets, *op. cit.*, p. 674.

2 & 3 King, *op. cit.*, pp. 186, 189, 191.

4 See notes to *Telegraph*, line 6. The interpolating index for net income between 1912 and 1917 is the net income reported by sample corporations.

TRADE
1 King, *op. cit.*, p. 122.

2 Unpublished data underlying the estimates in *ibid.*

3 *1914-18:* difference between total and corporate savings (for the latter see note to line 6). Total savings are obtained by raising corporate by the ratio of total sales to corporate (available for 1919 in the data underlying estimates for 1919-38 and extrapolated back to 1914 by the manufacturing ratio of total value of product to corporate).
1919-21: Kuznets, *op. cit.*, p. 312.

Appendix Table III 9 continued: TRADE *(concl.)*

LINE

4 & 5 Unpublished data underlying the estimates in King, *op. cit.*

6 *1916-18:* the difference between corporate net income after taxes (*Statistics of Income*) and dividends paid (see line 4). For 1914 and 1915 corporate savings are extrapolated from 1916 with sample corporate data as index.

1919-21: Kuznets, *op. cit.*, p. 312.

7 Sum of lines 1 through 6.

For 1920 and 1921, lines 1, 2, and 5: King's total payments for 1920 and 1921 were adjusted to the trend of the estimates in *National Income and Its Composition,* i.e., the ratio of total payments for trade to aggregate payments, computed for 1919 from King's data, was extrapolated for 1920-21 by the similar ratio for Kuznets' data. The various types of payment within the group were based on the revised total payments and King's original percentage distribution of payments, by type, on the assumption that dividends, as computed by King, were correct.

BANKING

1 & 2 King, *op. cit.*, pp. 122, 191.

3 *1914-18: Income in the United States,* Vol. 2, p. 236.

1919-21: Kuznets, *op. cit.*, p. 736.

4 Sum of lines 1 through 3.

GOVERNMENT

1 King, *op. cit.*, p. 138.

2 Difference between lines 1 and 3.

3 King, *op. cit.*, p. 122.

4 *Ibid.*, p. 370.

5 Sum of lines 3 and 4.

UNCLASSIFIED

1 Wages and salaries reported in King, *op. cit.*, p. 122, plus wages and salaries transferred from manufacturing (see notes to *Manufacturing,* line 1) minus wages and salaries for manufactured gas (see notes to *Electric Light and Power and Manufactured Gas,* line 1). A further adjustment is made for 1920 and 1921 (see notes to *Trade*).

2 Difference between realized income of entrepreneurs and property holders (King, *op. cit.*, p. 108) and rent paid (unpublished estimates underlying the data in *ibid.*). An adjustment is made for 1920 and 1921 (see notes to *Trade*).

3 *1914-18:* difference between total (see notes to *Construction,* lines 3 and 4) and corporate sav-
& ings. The division into entrepreneurial and corporate savings is based on the division of total
5 net profits into those of entrepreneurs and corporations calculated from unpublished data underlying the estimates in King, *op. cit.*

1919-21: Kuznets, *op. cit.*, p. 312 (difference between the total and the specified industries).

4 King, *op. cit.*, p. 379.

6 Sum of lines 1 through 5.

RENT PAID

1 The sum of unpublished estimates underlying the data in King, *op. cit.*, it includes rent paid by agriculture, mining, manufacturing, steam railroads, Pullman, and express, street railways, telephone, telegraph, trade, and unclassified industries, and rent of leased dwellings.

INCOME PAYMENTS-BUSINESS SAVINGS AGGREGATE

1-3, 5, 8, 9, 10 Sum of items shown above for specific industries.

4 Realized income of entrepreneurs and property holders (King, *op. cit.*, p. 108) minus interest payments (line 7, below), interest paid by banks (unpublished), dividends (line 6, below), rent paid (*Rent,* line 1), agricultural savings (*Agriculture,* line 3), miscellaneous income other than rent paid on leased dwellings (King, *op. cit.*, p. 379) and imputed rent on owner-occupied farm dwellings (unpublished).

6 See *ibid.*, pp. 189, 191.

7 Interest paid by corporations (*ibid.*, p. 186) plus agricultural interest (*Agriculture*, line 4) plus government interest (*Government*, line 4).

11 Sum of lines 3 through 10.

APPENDIX TABLE III 10

This table provides the basis data for the analysis in Table III 6 of the text. Two aspects of the estimates should be noted. First, for World War I the number employed is reduced to full-time units in the industries for which it is possible to do so; for World War II it is not. Second, the figures for government include employees of government owned and operated arsenals and shipyards.

APPENDIX TABLE III 10

Total Engaged, by Industry, World Wars I and II
(millions)

A WORLD WAR I

	1914	1915	1916	1917	1918	1919
1 Agriculture, employees	2.2	2.2	2.2	2.2	2.2	2.3
2 Agriculture, entrepreneurs	6.4	6.4	6.4	6.4	6.4	6.4
3 Agriculture, total (1 + 2)	8.5	8.6	8.5	8.6	8.6	8.7
4 Mining, employees	1.1	1.1	1.1	1.2	1.2	1.2
5 Mining, entrepreneurs	0.03	0.03	0.03	0.02	0.02	0.02
6 Mining, total (4 + 5)	1.2	1.1	1.2	1.2	1.2	1.2
7 Manufacturing, employees	7.4	7.5	8.8	9.5	9.9	9.9
8 Manufacturing, entrepreneurs	0.2	0.2	0.2	0.2	0.2	0.2
9 Manufacturing, total (7 + 8)	7.7	7.7	9.0	9.7	10.2	10.1
10 Construction, employees	1.0	1.0	1.0	1.0	0.8	1.0
11 Construction, entrepreneurs	0.2	0.2	0.2	0.2	0.2	0.2
12 Construction, total (10 + 11)	1.2	1.2	1.2	1.1	0.9	1.2
13 Transp. & other pub. util., employees	2.7	2.7	2.8	2.9	3.1	3.2
14 Transp. & other pub. util., entrepreneurs	0.03	0.03	0.03	0.03	0.03	0.03
15 Transp. & other pub. util., total (13 + 14)	2.8	2.7	2.8	3.0	3.1	3.3
16 Trade, employees	2.7	2.8	2.9	2.9	2.9	3.0
17 Trade, entrepreneurs	1.3	1.3	1.4	1.4	1.3	1.4
18 Trade, total (16 + 17)	4.0	4.1	4.3	4.3	4.2	4.4
19 Government, employees	1.9	2.0	2.1	2.7	5.2	3.8
20 Unclassified, employees	7.9	8.3	8.4	7.5	5.5	5.5
21 Unclassified, entrepreneurs	1.8	1.8	1.8	1.8	1.7	1.8
22 Unclassified, total (20 + 21)	9.8	10.1	10.2	9.4	7.2	7.2
23 Total	37.0	37.5	39.3	40.0	40.6	39.8

Appendix Table III 10 continued:

B WORLD WAR II

		1939	1940	1941	1942	1943
1	Agricultural	9.40	9.30	8.64	8.64	8.28
2	Nonagricultural	35.75	37.10	40.45	43.47	44.14
3	Wage & salary excl. domestic service	30.35	31.78	35.67	38.45	39.72
4	Domestic	2.33	2.30	2.20	2.15	1.69
5	Other (2 — 3 — 4)	3.07	3.02	2.58	2.87	2.73
6	Mining, wage & salary	.84	.92	.95	.97	.89
7	Mining, other (0.8% of line 5)	.02	.03	.02	.02	.02
8	Mining, total (6 + 7)	.86	.95	.97	.99	.91
9	Manufacturing, wage & salary	10.08	10.78	12.97	15.05	16.92
10	Manufacturing, other (5.9% of line 5)	.18	.18	.15	.17	.16
11	Manufacturing, total (9 + 10)	10.26	10.96	13.12	15.22	17.08
12	Construction, wage & salary	1.75	1.72	2.24	2.08	1.26
13	Construction, other (10.3% of line 5)	.32	.31	.26	.30	.28
14	Construction, total (12 + 13)	2.07	2.03	2.50	2.38	1.54
15	Transp. & other pub. util., wage & salary	2.91	3.01	3.25	3.43	3.62
16	Transp. & other pub. util., other (4.1% of line 5)	.13	.12	.11	.12	.11
17	Transp. & other pub. util., total (15 + 16)	3.04	3.13	3.36	3.55	3.73
18	Trade, wage & salary	6.62	6.91	7.38	7.26	7.03
19	Trade, other (44.8% of line 5)	1.37	1.35	1.16	1.28	1.23
20	Trade, total (18 + 19)	7.99	8.26	8.54	8.54	8.26
21	Gov., wage & salary, civilian	3.99	4.14	4.45	5.20	5.89
22	Finance, service, & misc., wage & salary (excl. domestic service)	4.16	4.31	4.44	4.45	4.12
23	Finance, service, & misc., other (34.1% of line 5)	1.05	1.03	.88	.98	.93
24	Finance, service, & misc., total excl. domestic service (22 + 23)	5.21	5.34	5.32	5.43	5.05
25	Finance, service, & misc., total incl. domestic service (4 + 24)	7.54	7.64	7.52	7.58	6.74
26	Total employed, civilian (1 + 2)	45.15	46.40	49.09	52.11	52.42
27	Armed forces	.40	.60	1.70	4.20	8.90
28	Total employed (26 + 27)	45.55	47.00	50.79	56.31	61.32

LINE   PART A

1 Unpublished data underlying the estimates of the number of employees attached in King, *National Income and Its Purchasing Power,* Tables IV and V, pp. 56 and 60.

2 *Ibid.,* Table VI, p. 62.

4 See notes to line 1.

5 King, *op. cit.,* Table VI, p. 62.

7 King's unpublished estimates of the number at work, revised to exclude (1) employees in railroad repair shops (a duplicated item); (2) employees in manufactured gas (transferred to public utilities); and (3) power laundry employees (covered in unclassified).

8 King, *op. cit.,* Table VI, p. 62.

10 See note to line 1.

11 King, *op. cit.,* Table VI, p. 62.

13 See note to line 1. Estimates of manufactured gas employees are added.

14 Unpublished estimates underlying those in King, *op. cit.,* Table VI, p. 62.

16 See note to line 1.

LINE

17 King, *op. cit.*, Table VI, p. 62.

19 See note to line 1.

20 Total labor force is given in Clarence D. Long's 'The Labor Force in Wartime America', National Bureau *Occasional Paper 14,* March 1944, p. 40.

Employees attached to unclassified are estimated by subtracting from this total (1) the number of entrepreneurs (lines 2, 5, 8, 11, 14, 17, and 21) and (2) the number of employees attached to specific industries. The latter for agriculture, mining, construction, trade, and government are given in King, *op. cit.,* Tables IV and V, pp. 56 and 60; for manufacturing and transportation and other public utilities, estimated on the assumption that the percentage of unemployment was the same as King used. Multiplying the number attached to unclassified by the ratio of employed to attached for agriculture, mining, manufacturing, construction, transportation and other public utilities, and trade yields the number of employees engaged in the unclassified industries.

21 King, *op. cit.,* Table VI, p. 62. The total reported minus entrepreneurs in transportation included in Unclassified in Table VI plus entrepreneurs in banking shown separately.

Part B

1 & 2 The estimates for 1940-43 are from the Census *Monthly Report on the Labor Force,* June 13, 1944. The 1939 data are comparable estimates based on BLS and BAE data.

3, 6, 9, 12, 15, 18, 21, 22 BLS estimates as given in BLS release LS44-4087 (May 29, 1944). The government estimates include employees at government arsenals and shipyards.

4 Based on unpublished Census tabulations of the labor force survey data adjusted to the 1940 decennial census.

7, 10, 13, 16, 19, 23 Line 5 distributed proportionately to the distribution of self-employed and unpaid family workers as reported in the 1940 decennial census.

27 *1939-42:* the estimates are from S. M. Livingston, 'Post-war Manpower and Its Capacity to Produce', *Survey of Current Business,* April 1943, p. 10, Table 1.

1943: it is an average of the monthly figures from January through November (*Occasional Paper 14,* p. 68) and the January 1, 1944 figure (*Survey,* Feb. 1944, p. 5, Table 5).

Appendix Table III 11

In this table physical output indexes are assembled for as many industries as are covered by data for both wars. No attempt has been made to include indexes that are available for recent years alone.

The comparison of indexes of physical output with gross national product in constant prices is subject to one major qualification: a larger increase in the physical output of an industry than in national product in constant prices does not necessarily mean that the share of the net value product of the industry, in real terms, increases relative to the net product of the economy. Physical output indexes measure the full gross value product of an industry, and an increase in it may be due to a bigger draft by the industry upon other industries. In other words, in any given industry the ratio of net value product (or of some gross value product short of the full value of output) to the full value of output need not remain constant over time.

It is doubtful, however, that changes in this ratio can be substantial during brief periods, especially for industrial categories as comprehensive as those in Appendix Table III 11. So long as comparisons are confined to categories as comprehensive and to periods as brief as those in this table, the qualification is not of great moment.

APPENDIX TABLE III 11
Physical Production Indexes, Major Industrial Divisions
World Wars I and II

WORLD WAR I (1914 = 100)

	1914	1915	1916	1917	1918
1 Agriculture	100	100	92	96	101
2 Mining	100	109	126	133	134
3 Manufacturing	100	117	139	138	137
4 Construction	100	89	91	93	94.5
5 Transportation					
a) Railroad	100	107	124	136	142
6 Gross national product (1914 prices)	100	108	114	120	115

WORLD WAR II (1939 = 100)

	1939	1940	1941	1942	1943
7 Agriculture	100	103	106	117	122
8 Mining	100	110	118	122	125
9 Manufacturing	100	116	154	194	237
10 Construction	100	114	168	191	104
11 Transportation: Total	100	108	134	169	202
a) Railroad	100	110	139	192	231
12 Gross national product (1939 prices)	100	109	127	138	161

LINE

1 & 2 Harold Barger and S. H. Schurr, *The Mining Industries, 1899-1939: A Study of Output, Employment and Productivity* (National Bureau of Economic Research, 1944), p. 14.

3 Solomon Fabricant, *Employment in Manufacturing, 1899-1939: An Analysis of Its Relation to the Volume of Production* (National Bureau of Economic Research, 1942), p. 331.

4 Deflated dollar figures of the value of new construction (including publicly-financed) in 1915 prices for 1915-18 are from unpublished worksheets of the Bureau of Foreign and Domestic Commerce.

   The total value of construction was deflated by components; military construction is included.

LINE

The 1914 figure is an extrapolation of the 1915 figure (unpublished BFDC worksheet) by the 1914 and 1915 values of the index of the physical volume of new construction plotted on Figure 8, p. 33, of L. J. Chawner's *Construction Activity in the United States, 1915-37* (Domestic Commerce Series 99).

5 The index compiled by W. W. Stewart (*American Economic Review*, Vol. 11, p. 68, 1921) was used. The transportation index, 'total transportation', consists of two parts: freight, measured in ton-miles; and passenger, measured in passenger-miles. They were combined by using the 1914 value added as weights; but how the total value added by the railroad industry was divided between freight and passenger is not described.

6 Based on Table III 1, line 3.

7 Index of the physical volume of farm marketings prepared by the Bureau of Agricultural Economics and the Bureau of Foreign and Domestic Commerce, given for 1939-42 in the *Survey of Current Business*, April 1943, p. 24, Table 1, and calculated for 1943 from the monthly data published in subsequent issues.

8 The 'minerals' component of the Federal Reserve Board index of industrial production is used (the latest revision is described in the *Federal Reserve Bulletin*, Oct. 1943). Covering three fuels and six metals, it is computed by using as weights the average value of production in 1935-39. Failure to include the newer metals and retention of gold and silver at the old weights undoubtedly lead to an understatment of the impact of the war on mining.

9 Same source and method of weighting as in line 8. The Federal Reserve Board index, as revised in October 1943, comprises some 95 individual series in the 'manufactures' component, of which 32 represent durable manufactures. Products not readily measurable in physical terms are included in the index by substituting man hours figures corrected for productivity changes.

10 Deflated dollar figures on the value of new construction in 1939 prices were computed as follows: an implicit price index was obtained by dividing estimates of private construction in current prices (*Survey of Current Business*, April 1944) by Department of Commerce estimates in 1939 prices; this index was then used to deflate estimates of total new construction (*ibid.*, June 1943 and monthly thereafter). From this deflated construction series the construction index was computed. Revisions of the construction data, which appeared in the June 1944 *Survey of Current Business*, do not warrant recalculation of the index.

11 The index for the total, representing commercial forms of transportation as calculated by the Bureau of Foreign and Domestic Commerce (*Survey of Current Business*, May 1943 and subsequent issues), is based on ton-miles for 5 types of commodity transportation (railroad, water, inter-city motor truck and bus, air, and oil and gas pipelines) and passenger-miles for 4 types of passenger transportation (railroad, intercity motor bus, local transit lines, and air). Ton- and passenger-miles are weighted according to the proportion of operating revenues for each type of transportation in the base period, 1935-39. The index of railroad transportation, a component of the BFDC index of total transportation includes both commodity and passenger transportation. It too is published monthly in the *Survey*.

12 Based on Table III 1, line 6b.

Index

Relation of the Directors to the Work and Publications

of the

National Bureau of Economic Research

1. The object of the National Bureau of Economic Research is to ascertain and to present to the public important economic facts and their interpretation in a scientific and impartial manner. The Board of Directors is charged with the responsibility of ensuring that the work of the Bureau is carried on in strict conformity with this object.

2. To this end the Board of Directors shall appoint one or more Directors of Research.

3. The Director or Directors of Research shall submit to the members of the Board, or to its Executive Committee, for their formal adoption, all specific proposals concerning researches to be instituted.

4. No report shall be published until the Director or Directors of Research shall have submitted to the Board a summary drawing attention to the character of the data and their utilization in the report, the nature and treatment of the problems involved, the main conclusions and such other information as in their opinion would serve to determine the suitability of the report for publication in accordance with the principles of the Bureau.

5. A copy of any manuscript proposed for publication shall also be submitted to each member of the Board. For each manuscript to be so submitted a special committee shall be appointed by the President, or at his designation by the Executive Director, consisting of three Directors selected as nearly as may be one from each general division of the Board. The names of the special manuscript committee shall be stated to each Director when the summary and report described in paragraph (4) are sent to him. It shall be the duty of each member of the committee to read the manuscript. If each member of the special committee signifies his approval within thirty days, the manuscript may be published. If each member of the special committee has not signified his approval within thirty days of the transmittal of the report and manuscript, the Director of Research shall then notify each member of the Board, requesting approval or disapproval of publication, and thirty additional days shall be granted for this purpose. The manuscript shall then not be published unless at least a majority of the entire Board and a two-thirds majority of those members of the Board who shall have voted on the proposal within the time fixed for the receipt of votes on the publication proposed shall have approved.

6. No manuscript may be published, though approved by each member of the special committee, until forty-five days have elapsed from the transmittal of the summary and report. The interval is allowed for the receipt of any memorandum of dissent or reservation, together with a brief statement of his reasons, that any member may wish to express; and such memorandum of dissent or reservation shall be published with the manuscript if he so desires. Publication does not, however, imply that each member of the Board has read the manuscript, or that either members of the Board in general, or of the special committee, have passed upon its validity in every detail.

7. A copy of this resolution shall, unless otherwise determined by the Board, be printed in each copy of every National Bureau book.

(Resolution adopted October 25, 1926 and revised February 6, 1933 and February 24, 1941)

Publications

BOOKS

aListed also as the first volume under Studies in Business Cycles.
*Out of print.

25 *German Business Cycles, 1924-1933* (1934)
C. T. Schmidt   288 pp., $2.50
26 *Industrial Profits in the United States* (1934)
R. C. Epstein   678 pp., $5.00
27 *Mechanization in Industry* (1934)
Harry Jerome   484 pp., $3.50
28 *Corporate Profits as Shown by Audit Reports* (1935)
W. A. Paton   151 pp., $1.25
29 *Public Works in Prosperity and Depression* (1935)
A. D. Gayer   460 pp., $3.00
30 *Ebb and Flow in Trade Unionism* (1936)
Leo Wolman   251 pp., $2.50
31 *Prices in Recession and Recovery* (1936)
Frederick C. Mills   561 pp., $4.00
32 *National Income and Capital Formation, 1919-1935* (1937)
Simon Kuznets   100 pp., 8¼ x 11¾, $1.50
33 *Some Theoretical Problems Suggested by the Movements of Interest
Rates, Bond Yields and Stock Prices in the United States Since 1856*
(1938), F. R. Macaulay   586 pp., $5.00
The Social Sciences and the Unknown Future, a reprint of the intro-
ductory chapter to Dr. Macaulay's volume: 35 cents; in orders of 10 or
more, 25 cents.
*34 *Commodity Flow and Capital Formation*, Volume 1 (1938)
Simon Kuznets
*35 *Capital Consumption and Adjustment* (1938)
Solomon Fabricant
36 *The Structure of Manufacturing Production, A Cross-Section View*
(1939)
C. A. Bliss   234 pp., $2.50
37 *The International Gold Standard Reinterpreted, 1914-34* (1940)
William Adams Brown, Jr.   2 vol., 1420 pp., $12.00
38 *Residential Real Estate, Its Economic Position as Shown by Values,
Rents, Family Incomes, Financing, and Construction, Together with
Estimates for All Real Estate* (1941)
D. L. Wickens   320 pp., 8¼ x 11¾, $3.50
39 *The Output of Manufacturing Industries, 1899-1937* (1940)
Solomon Fabricant   700 pp., $4.50
*40 *National Income and Its Composition, 1919-1938* (1941)
Simon Kuznets
41 *Employment in Manufacturing, 1899-1939: An Analysis of its Relation
to the Volume of Production* (1942)
Solomon Fabricant   360 pp., $3.00
42 *American Agriculture, 1899-1939: A Study of Output, Employment
and Productivity* (1942)
Harold Barger and Hans H. Landsberg   435 pp., $3.00

*Out of print.

*Out of print.

*Out of print.

Occasional Papers

*Out of print.

TECHNICAL PAPERS